美 國 淨 宗 學 會
AMITABHA BUDDHIST SOCIETY OF U.S.A.
650 S. BERNARDO AVENUE
SUNNYVALE, CA 94087, U.S.A.
TEL: (408)736-3386   FAX: (408)736-3389
http://www.amtb-usa.org

NAMO AMITABHA

南無阿彌陀佛

真誠 清淨 平等 正覺 慈悲

看破 放下 自在 隨緣 念佛

To Understand Buddhism

Given by Venerable Master Chin Kung
Excerpts from the Talk
Australia
January 1996

Translated by Silent Voices

This Book is Authorized to the Public for Reproduction and Free Distribution

First Edition 1998: October 1998
10,000 Copies

Reprinted for free distribution by
**The Corporate Body of
the Buddha Educational Foundation**
11F. 55, Hang Chow South Road. Sec 1,
Taipei, Taiwan, R.O.C.
Tel: 886-2-3951198 , Fax: 886-2-3913415
1999 September, 37500 Copies

Dedication

This book is dedicated to all the beings
in the ten directions,
in the present and in the future,
who have not yet been born into
Buddha Amitabha's Western Pure Land.

Table of Contents

Table of Contents

"To Understand Buddhism"
Excerpts from the Talk
Australia
January, 1996

Chapter One: A Virtuous and Perfect Education

Today, we see an increasing number of people around the world starting to practice Buddhism. However, not many people truly understand what Buddhism is. Therefore, this becomes a very important topic. What exactly is Buddhism? We need to understand it clearly. Buddhism is a most virtuous and perfect education directed by the Buddha towards all sentient beings in the nine realms. How can we tell that Buddhism is an education? First, we can tell from the way we call Buddha Shakyamuni our "Original Teacher" that he is the founder of Buddhism and that we are his students. From this, it is very apparent that the Buddha and we share a teacher-student relationship. This is only found in education.

If Buddhism is his teaching, who then is the Buddha? Buddha is a Sanskrit word meaning wisdom and enlightenment. However, this wisdom is not the worldly wisdom we think of today. Broadly speaking, the Buddha's wisdom is the ability to ultimately, perfectly and correctly comprehend the true reality of life and the universe in the past, present and future. One who has perceived this wisdom is called a Buddha. Buddha Shakyamuni told us that all sentient beings, including ourselves, possess this innate wisdom and ability. Thus Buddhism regards all beings equally. Although we are equal in origin, presently we cannot see this because everyone's wisdom and abilities differ.

In our society, there are those who are intelligent and those who are not, those with great ability and those with less. How do these things come about? The Buddha told us that they are due to our varying degrees of delusion. Our innate wisdom and abilities are temporarily lost due to this delusion, but are not truly or permanently lost. If we can break through this delusion, then we will be able to recover these abilities. Therefore, the Buddha's teachings show us how to rid ourselves of delusion and to uncover our innate abilities.

It is often stated in Mahayana sutras that the Buddha did not directly help sentient beings. Then how do sentient beings become Buddhas? By themselves. The Buddha only assists from the side by explaining the true reality of how we delude ourselves. After realizing this, we diligently put his teachings into practice to attain enlightenment of true reality. We then become Buddhas. Buddha Shakyamuni clearly explained that becoming a Buddha is attainable by all sentient beings.

From this, we can see that Buddhism is a teaching. However, a teacher can only educate us about the principles, tell us of his/her experiences in practice and attainment, and suggest various methods for our attainment. The rest ultimately depends upon us. We are the ones who need to be enthusiastic and diligent in order to attain achievement. Once we understand that Buddhism is an education, we will logically regard the Buddha as our teacher. From this, we understand that in proper Way Places, we do not regard the Buddha or Bodhisattva images as gods to be worshipped. We make offerings to these images for two reasons. First, to remember and repay our gratitude for this truly great education, which we have so fortunately encountered and accepted in this lifetime.

The opening verse to sutras says it very well; "It is extremely difficult to encounter this teaching in infinite eons." The debt of gratitude we owe the Buddha is similar to the remembrance, which some Chinese have toward their ancestors. We reflect on our origins for without these ancestors we would not exist. The second reason we make offerings to the Buddha is to follow the examples of the virtuous. Buddha Shakyamuni was an ordinary person like us; yet, he was able to be awakened and become a Buddha. What is there to stop us from achieving this as well? Therefore, the pictures or statues of the Buddha serve to remind us every moment to advance diligently towards this goal. The images are not to be regarded as gods or objects of superstition.

In Buddhist Way Places, the images of

Buddhas and Bodhisattvas have many appearances. This has often led to the misconception that not only is Buddhism a religion but one that worships multi-deities as well. Indeed Buddhas and Bodhisattvas have many names. For example, in the Tripitaka there is the <u>Ten Thousand-Buddha Names Sutra,</u> which gives us over twelve thousand Buddha's names and even more names for Bodhisattvas. Why are there so many Buddhas and Bodhisattvas? Within our original-nature there exists infinite wisdom, virtuous and artistic abilities that cannot be completely represented by merely one name. It is similar to a highly accomplished person in a prominent position; his or her business card could have numerous titles.

The names of the Buddhas represent the complete, innate and virtuous abilities within our self-nature. All the Bodhisattva names represent cultivation of different virtues. The original abilities within our self-nature are infinite, but temporarily lost. Without genuine cultivation, we will not be able to uncover any of them. All the Buddha and Bodhisattva names are none other than ourselves. Once we understand this, we will realize that a high level of artistry represents the styles of the Buddha's teachings. For example, sculptures and pictures can express the Dharma. Understanding the true meaning of these images will help one to gain the true benefits of the Buddha's teachings.

If Buddhism is not a religion, why is it not then a philosophy? In philosophy, there is both a subject and an object. In Mahayana Buddhism, there is no difference between subject and object; they are one. This meaning is very profound and difficult to understand. For example, a great master said, "Utilizing gold to form utensils, all utensils are of gold." Are the gold and the utensil the same thing or different? From their appearances they look like two different things. However, from their composition we realize that they are the same.

One needs a profound intuitive comprehension to truly understand the reality of life and the universe. All of the Mahayana Sutras try to explain this concept and truth. One will share the same viewpoints with the Buddha when one truly understands and clearly recognizes this truth. Ordinary people, like we are deluded. In what way? Because we see everything in opposition to the other, not knowing that in reality everything is actually one and not two.

Chapter Two: The Goal of the Buddha's Teaching

From the intrinsic nature of Buddhism, we proceed to the goal of the Buddha's teachings. This goal is to break through delusion and achieve enlightenment. The Buddha pointed out to us why we are leading lives of suffering and why the six realms of reincarnation exist. It is so, because the wisdom and virtuous abilities in our original nature have yet to be uncovered. Thus, all our viewpoints and ways of interacting with life and the universe are incorrect. The erroneous acts committed due to these incorrect viewpoints and ways have resulted in the suffering of reincarnation within the six realms.

The goal of the Buddha's teachings is to help and to guide us break through our delusion, to be awakened and to escape this suffering and obtain happiness. What do we seek in Buddhism? We seek Annut-tara-Samyak-Sambodhi, the Perfect Complete Enlightenment. The Buddha teaches and hopes that all of us will attain this ultimate enlightenment, in other words, will become a Buddha.

The Perfect Complete Enlightenment can be explained as three levels: Arhats, Bodhisattvas and Buddhas. The first is *"Proper Enlightenment."* In our world, there are some very intelligent and wise people, such as scientists, philosophers and religious leaders. They have reached higher realization than most people have. However, although they may have reached a certain level of realization, the Buddha would not recognize their knowl-edge as the proper enlightenment, be-cause they have not severed their afflic-tions. They still dwell on the rights and wrongs of others, on greed, anger, igno-rance and arrogance. They still harbor wandering, discriminatory thoughts and attachments. In other words, their minds are not pure. Without the pure mind, no matter how high the level of realization one reaches, it is still not the proper enlightenment.

In Buddhism, the standard for proper enlightenment is the pure mind from which wisdom arises. It is the wish of all Buddhas that we attain this proper enlightenment. This is the level or degree of an Arhat and is similar to attending a university to earn an undergraduate degree. Therefore, Arhat, Bodhisattva and Buddha are titles similar to degrees of enlightenment attained in Buddhism. Those who achieve proper enlightenment are called Arhats. Arhats do not have illusory or misleading thoughts and viewpoints. They do not dwell on the rights and wrongs of others, or on thoughts of greed, anger, ignorance or arrogance.

From this, we can comprehend intuitively the difference between Buddhism and worldly education. From the Buddha, we learn the true teachings and proper enlightenment. Only with this proper enlightenment can one escape all sufferings to obtain true happiness. As human beings, we undergo the sufferings of birth, old age, sickness and death. We do not attain what we seek, are parted with our loved ones and find ourselves in the presence of those whom we resent or even hate. We are surrounded by all these sufferings with no apparent way of being truly free. Only after learning Buddhism will we be able to reach genuine liberation.

The <u>Flower Adornment Sutra</u> explains to us, "All sentient beings possess the same wisdom and virtuous capabilities as the Buddha, but these qualities are unattainable due to wandering thoughts and attachments." This clearly explains the root cause of our problems. Practicing Buddhism is to accord with the teachings of the Buddha, to rid us of wandering, discriminating thoughts and attachments. Thus, we uncover our pure mind, in turn giving rise to true wisdom, which is proper enlightenment. Therefore, Buddhas and Bodhisattvas would not recognize the intelligent and worldly wisdom, as it lacks the pure mind, the proper enlightenment. Upon attaining proper enlightenment, one has the ability to transcend the endless cycles of birth and death, not to mention the ability to solve everyday problems.

Whether talking about the Buddha's education or worldly education, it is essential to understand the concept of delving deeply into one method in order to attain achievement. This is especially so in Buddhism. One who truly wishes to learn effectively needs to follow only one teacher and practice only one path to ensure a smooth journey. When following two teachers with two different paths, one is bound to become confused as to which path to take. Even worse, following three teachers catches one at a T street. With four teachers one is caught at a cross street. Today's young people like to learn a lot, but fail to attain a good result. The problem lies with being caught at those cross streets, confused as to which way to take. For one to succeed and attain achievement in practicing Buddhism, one needs to follow just one teacher and concentrate on just one method.

What is this achievement? True achievement is attaining a pure mind. Upon achieving some degree of pure mind, one will have fewer afflictions and thus an increase in true wisdom, enabling one to solve problems in this world and beyond. Without this true wisdom, there is no way to truly solve problems. Therefore, true wisdom is essential in leading a happy and fulfilling life. On a broader scale, it can help us to solve society's problems.

Today there are many intelligent politicians who thought they were very smart but have ended up bringing their countries to the brink of disaster, as well as putting their citizens through much misery. What is the reason for this? These leaders have not severed their afflictions, discriminating and wandering thoughts, and attachments. Consequently, their first consideration is their own benefit, their self-attachment.

The Buddha taught us to attain true wisdom by first breaking free of our own viewpoints. Without this wisdom, one could misinterpret the meanings within the Mahayana sutras. If one is able to part from the selfish mind, then true benefits will definitely be received. With proper enlightenment, only when one has no ego or self-attachment, will one be able to differentiate true from false, proper from deviated, right from wrong and beneficial from harmful. Without breaking through one's own viewpoints, one will not have these abilities. From this, we understand there is a standard to the proper enlightenment.

One level above the proper enlightenment is the *"Equal and Proper Enlightenment."* Equal means equal to the Buddha, but not yet having become a Buddha. This level is higher than that of an Arhat. The equal and proper enlightenment requires one to break through one degree of ignorance, to attain one degree of Dharma body. At this point, the way one views the reality of life and the universe is very close to that of the Buddhas. One who achieves the equal and proper enlightenment would be called a Bodhisattva.

The <u>Flower Adornment Sutra</u> explains the forty-one levels of Bodhisattvas, all of which have these levels of enlightenment. After breaking through the very last degree of ignorance, perfecting wisdom and enlightenment, one achieves the *"Perfect, Complete Enlightenment"* that is Buddhahood. Therefore, Buddha, Bodhisattva and Arhat are common titles, not a specific name for a specific person. They are titles similar to those of Doctorate, Master or Graduate degrees. For example, in the name Guan Yin Bodhisattva, Guan Yin represents great compassion and kindness. The title of Bodhisattva is similar to a Masters Degree. Presently, people have misconceptions about Buddhas and Bodhisattvas, thinking these names are specific beings. They do not understand that these titles refer to any being who possesses those characteristics. Buddha or Bodhisattva, when added to a name is simply referring to a specialty.

From the intrinsic nature of Buddhism, we realize that our purpose of practice is to seek wisdom. In Zen, this goal is called, "In pursuit of clarity of mind to see into one's self-nature." In other words "Complete Enlightenment." In the Pure Land School, this is called "One Mind Undisturbed." The Pure Land School is unique in that not only does one seek to have One Mind Undisturbed but also seeks birth into the Western Pure Land. This is unlike other schools, which rely on one's own strength of cultivation in seeking solely one goal. The Pure Land method has two goals that can be achieved in one lifetime.

One who is very familiar with the Infinite Life Sutra and understood its teachings would be free of doubt. The full title of this sutra reveals the goals of our practice: <u>The Buddha Speaks of the Infinite Life Sutra of Adornment, Purity, Equality and Enlightenment of the Mahayana School.</u> Infinite life and adornment are what Pure Land practitioners seek. *Infinite life* refers to the merits and virtues of one's perfect self-nature. *Adornment* refers to perfect complete wisdom with great ease and fulfillment. *Purity, equality* and *enlightenment* are the methods, the three ways of practice. Upon attaining any one, all three are attained. Of all the schools of Buddhism, none surpass these three ways of practice.

The Zen School uses the awakening path to reach the great enlightenment and attain the clarity to see into one's true nature. Buddhist schools other than Zen stress the practice of understanding or proper viewpoints, until reaching great complete understanding. The Pure Land School, on the other hand, concentrates on the pure mind. A person with purity of mind will naturally be non-discriminating and awakened. An awakened person will naturally have a pure and non-discriminating mind. The route chosen may be different but all reach the same goal. In Zen practice it is expressed as "obtaining clarity of mind and seeing into one's true nature."

Different schools may use different names but the results or the level of the state of mind are the same. Therefore, to criticize any other schools would be to slander both the Buddha and the Dharma. All these methods were passed down to us from Buddha Shakyamuni. Choosing any path will enable one to attain achievement. How can we say that one method is better than another? From all these different methods we just need to know how to choose the one method that is most suitable for us and our level.

First, if the level of the method we chose were beyond us, making it difficult to practice, we would not succeed easily with that method. Second, it needs to be suitable and convenient for our manner of living. Third, it needs to be compatible with modern society, because we cannot separate ourselves from society or other human beings. Therefore, we need to consider these factors to choose our method of cultivation.

However, no matter which method one practices, it is essential to be rid of self-viewpoint and attachment in order to obtain the benefits from practice. Or else, like so many have experienced, the great efforts put into the practice will have been in vain. Some practitioners have felt that even after years of practice they have achieved virtually nothing, even to the point of feeling that they were better off before they practiced. It seemed as if the more they practiced, the worse they felt. All this comes from having chosen a method that was unsuitable for them. This is similar to choosing an unsuitable major in school. When one chooses a major that is not suited to one's foundation and ability, one has an extremely difficult time trying to succeed. Choosing the right major makes studying much easier, so one will have a much better chance of success. The same thing goes for practicing Buddhism. If one does not know one's own capacity, one can test oneself.

Like myself, for example. After reading many Mahayana sutras, I thought myself incapable of any achievement. I wanted very much to sever my wandering, discriminating thoughts and attachments, but was unable to. Finally, I chose the Pure Land method to attain achievement. It does not require one to be completely rid of but rather to suppress these hindrances. As long as one is able to suppress all afflictions, one can still be born into the Western Pure Land carrying over one's existing karma.

This method suits me very well and thus is how I chose it. Previously, I had tried Zen, the Teaching Schools, the Esoteric School and the practice of following the precepts, but could not reach achievement with them. Thus, I came back to the Pure Land method and wholeheartedly delved deeply into the Buddha Name Chanting Method while concentrating solely on lecturing on the Pure Land sutras. These are my experiences from decades of practice.

Chapter Three: Symbolism and the Arts

After we understand clearly the goal of the Buddha's teachings, we will view the sutras differently. These sutras are one of the world's largest literary collections. I believe that when considering the range of all academia, none of them surpass Buddhism. To obtain the benefits from this vast collection, it is necessary for us to know and understand the essence of it's content, which is the true reality of all Dharma, the true reality of life and the universe. Life refers to ourselves. Universe refers to the living environment that surrounds us. It would be incorrect to treat Buddhism as an abstract and obscure learning that had nothing to do with our daily lives. Every word in the sutra closely relates to our daily living. Furthermore, it is definitely not superstition.

How and where do we start? For

convenience, the perfection in the methods of the Buddha's teaching, uses a high level of creativity. Buddhism of two thousand years ago had already taken an artistic path. For example, all the Buddha's names and sculptures represent our virtuous nature, innate qualities of wisdom, virtuous abilities and artistic talents. All of the Bodhisattva's names and forms represent our cultivation of virtue. They instruct us how to apply the teachings in our daily lives to bring out our virtuous nature so we may receive Buddhism's benefits.

In Chinese Mahayana Buddhism, four great Bodhisattvas represent our order of practice and level of achievement. The first is Earth Store Bodhisattva. Whether we are thinking of worldly teachings, the dharma or Buddhism; nothing can be accomplished without the earth or a place of existence. The existence of humans cannot be separated from our great earth as we rely upon it for survival. Whether clothing, food, living or working, all rely on the production of the land, thus the infinite treasures that the great earth encompasses are seemingly endless for us to use. The word "earth" in the name Earth Store Bodhisattva represents the mind and the word "store" means treasure.

The Buddha's teachings guide us to first start the practice from our mind, as our true nature encompasses the infinite wisdom and virtuous abilities that are no different from those of Buddhas or Bodhisattvas. However, today it seems as if we have lost our innate wisdom and virtuous abilities. The Buddha told us that all these qualities are not truly lost, just not yet uncovered. In the present moment, we endlessly immerse ourselves in wandering, discriminating thoughts and attachments, which have resulted in this temporary loss of abilities. However, inside the true mind, no wandering thoughts exist. If a mind has wandering thoughts then that mind is a false one. We originally possessed this true mind, so practicing Buddhism is simply recovering it. Therefore, our first goal in practice is to uncover and look for the treasure in our mind. In other words, the Buddha's teachings do not seek from the outside but rather they seek from within our self-nature.

Earth Store Bodhisattva represents filial piety; thus, the <u>Earth Store Sutra</u> is about filial piety, a basic concept that everyone would do well to start from. The kindness that our parents have shown by giving us life and nurturing us is beyond description. To be filial and take care of our parents is naturally our basic responsibility. Not only do we need to take care of their material needs but of their spiritual life as well. Moreover, we need to nurture their aspirations for us and for us, this is the hardest of all. Parents wish their children to have successful careers, behave well, and to be respected by current and future generations. In other words, we would do well to act in a manner, which will make them proud of us. Therefore, the ultimate and perfect achievement of filial piety is to become Buddha. We begin our practice from here and expand our filial piety and respect to include all sentient beings.

The second Bodhisattva, Guan Yin, represents the cultivation of great compassion and kindness. What is the meaning of making offerings to Guan Yin Bodhisattva? It is to remind us that we would do well to treat all people with great compassion and kindness, to use unconditional love and care to help all sentient beings.

The third Bodhisattva, Manjusri, represents wisdom and rationale, reminding us that when we practice and interact with others we need to fulfill our filial duty, to rely upon wisdom and rationale, not on emotion. The fourth Bodhisattva, the Great Samantabhadra (Universal Worthy) represents carrying out the cultivation truthfully, applying filial piety, compassion, kindness and rationale in our daily lives. When one perfectly achieves the way of Universal Worthy Bodhisattva, one becomes a Buddha. Buddhism teaches us how to live in harmony with the true reality of life and the universe. In other words, we would live perfect and wonderful lives similar to those of Buddhas and Bodhisattvas. This is the true, ultimate and perfect Mahayana teaching.

To practice Buddhism, we start by:

(1)   Being filial and respectful toward parents, teachers and elders,

(2)   Having the great compassionate mind,

(3) Nurturing one's thinking and wisdom and

(4) Broadening one's mind.

Although in sequence, they also can be practiced simultaneously, as each encompasses the others. For example, being filial to parents includes compassion and kindness, reasoning and wisdom. Wisdom includes being filial, compassionate and kind.

Once we have a general understanding of Buddhism, how do we apply it to our daily living? First we need to know what each Buddha and Bodhisattva represents. If we do not, then Buddhism would be reduced to superstition and we would not receive its true benefits. All Buddhist sutras contain these qualities, characteristics and the ways of practice; therefore, learning only one sutra will be enough. One needs to know how to understand and apply the teachings effectively.

Usually in the center of the main hall of a temple, there are statues of one Buddha and two Bodhisattvas, which represent our self-nature and original entity. The two Bodhisattvas represent our virtuous abilities within our self-nature; one is understanding and the other is practice. If the Buddha in the middle is Buddha Shakyamuni, then the two figures on either side of him will be Manjusri and Universal Worthy Bodhisattvas, representing wisdom and application respectively. Thus, understanding and practice are combined into one. If the hall has the three sages of Western Pure Land, with Buddha Amitabha in the middle, representing self-nature, then the two figures on either side of him will be Guan Yin and Great Strength Bodhisattvas. They respectively represent compassion and wisdom, completely symbolizing the infinite wisdom and virtuous capabilities. Therefore, we again see that Buddhism is a teaching.

There are profound teachings within the names of the Buddhas and Bodhisattvas, for example the name of Buddha Shakyamuni tells us the principles of the Buddha's education. "Shakya" means humanity and kindness. "Muni" means purity of mind. The teachings of these two qualities are advocated because people in our world lack compassion and kindness, and are often selfish. Moreover, all sentient beings lack purity of mind, constantly dwelling in wandering thoughts, greed, anger, ignorance and arrogance. Any Bodhisattva who becomes a Buddha in this world will be named Shakyamuni to teach us the remedy for our problems. Once the representations of Buddha and Bodhisattva statues are understood intuitively just by looking at them, one will perfectly comprehend the goal of the Buddha's teachings.

When we enter the first hall of a way place, the Hall of Heavenly Guardians, we will see the statue of Maitreya Bodhisattva surrounded by the four Heavenly Guardians in the middle of the hall. Maitreya Bodhisattva, known in the west as the Happy Buddha, has a huge smile representing joyfulness. His great stomach represents enormous tolerance and broad-mindedness, teaching us to interact with others and matters with joy, to be non-discriminating and tolerant. Next to him are four Heavenly Guardians or Dharma Protectors who teach us how to protect ourselves.

The Eastern Dharma Protector, symbolizes fulfilling one's duty and responsibility, teaching us that regardless of position, one needs to fulfill one's duties. He is holding a lute in his hand. The strings of the instrument should not be too tight, or else they will break; nor should they be too loose or they will not play well. When properly adjusted and balanced, the instrument will play beautifully, clearly symbolizing that we need to take the middle path when interacting with matters, people and objects. When each of us fulfills our responsibilities and obligations, how could the nation not prosper?

The Southern Dharma Protector symbolizes improvement and daily advancement. Not only do matters need to be taken care of appropriately; continuous improvement also needs to be sought. In his right hand, the Southern Dharma Protector holds the sword of wisdom and in his left hand a ring symbolizing the perfection of wisdom, showing us that one needs to use wisdom in seeking improvement. The sword symbolizes how one needs to sever afflictions before they are out of control.

The third and fourth Heavenly Guardians are the Western and the Northern Dharma Protectors, representing comprehensive vision and listening respectively. Both teach us to observe and listen more carefully as well as to read numerous books and travel to many places for comprehensive learning. They teach us to do well in our job, to adopt the good qualities as well as to disregard the shortcomings of others.

The Western Dharma Protector represents far-sighted observation and holds a dragon or snake. The dragon or snake symbolizes constant change. In his other hand, he holds a bead, symbolizing principles. People, matters and objects in society undergo changes constantly. One needs to observe very carefully and thoroughly, to have a firm grasp on the principles within in order to be able to control this "dragon or snake." The Northern Dharma Protector holds an umbrella to prevent one from being contaminated. This reminds us that within a complex society, one needs to know how to protect one's body and mind from pollution and corruption. From these examples, we can see that the artistic aspects of the Buddha's education are truly beautiful. Unfortunately, many people regard these Dharma protectors as gods to be worshipped, which is totally wrong.

Chapter Four: The Five Guidelines of Practice

The Three Conditions

After establishing Pure Land Learning Centers in several countries, we set five guidelines for Pure Land practitioners to follow. These five guidelines were extracted from the five Pure Land sutras to be applied in daily living. The first guideline is the Three Conditions, extracted from the <u>Visualization Sutra</u>, which provides a very important foundation for cultivation. The Buddha stated in the sutra that these Three Conditions are the proper causes of which all the Buddhas from the past, present and future practice their pure karma. In other words, all the people who became Buddhas perfected these as their foundation; thus, we cannot disregard them.

The First Condition concerns the good

fortune of heavenly beings and humans. Before one can become a Buddha or a Bodhisattva, one needs to first become a good person. The criteria for this are:

(A)   Being filial and respectful toward parents, teachers, and elders,

(B)   Being compassionate and not killing any living being and

(C)   Practicing the Ten Good Conducts.

With this first step, we begin to practice Buddhism.

The Second Condition includes:

(A)   Taking the Three Refuges,

(B)   Abiding by laws, customs, and precepts,

(C)   Conducting oneself in proper and dignified manner.

The main principle of our practice is awakening, proper thoughts and viewpoints, and purity. A beginning step in learning Buddhism is to Take Refuge in the Triple Jewels. After one generates the heart to Take Refuge in the Triple Jewels by accepting, learning and practicing Buddhism, one finds a Dharma Master to pass on the principle, goal and direction of practicing Buddhism. The Triple Jewels are the Buddha, the Dharma and the Sangha. In appearance, they are pictures or sculptures of Buddhas, Buddhist sutras, and monks and nuns, respectively. Another way of understanding them is that they are the true Triple Jewels within our true mind.

The Buddha taught us to take refuge in the Triple Jewels of our self-nature. To return and rely upon the Buddha is to rely on the awakening in our self-nature. What is this awakening? Currently, we are deluded and not awakened. How did we become deluded? Delusion is due to our discriminating mind and attachments. If we part from this discriminating mind and attachments, can we still see objects clearly? We cannot say we do not see them, but if we see them very clearly without discriminating thoughts and attachments, then we are awakened. When there is the slightest discrimination or attachment, one is deluded.

The same applies to our attaching to the form we are looking at; it is delusion. Initially, objects do not have names but are given them by people. The names, like the object, are not real. Apart from the names and appearances, what we see is the true form. We are deluded about these forms, their physical features and their names. Consequently, when we rid ourselves of these delusions, we will not be attached. This is how we can train ourselves to return and rely upon the Buddha Jewel or Enlightenment.

If someone points to a table and asks what it is, we will naturally say it is a table because that is what everybody calls it. We go along with everybody's attachment but if we are not attached to it ourselves, then we will be awakened. Therefore, the minds of the Buddhas and Bodhisattvas are pure and without the slightest pollution for they are completely without these attachments. When with others, we can go along with them but maintain our purity inside. In this way, we return and rely upon awakening. After taking refuge, when we apply this concept to our daily living, whether interacting with people, matters or objects, we will no longer be deluded. Our mind will always be pure, non-discriminating and able to help all sentient beings. This is to return and rely upon awakening or the

Buddha Jewel.

The Dharma that we return to and rely upon refers to proper thoughts and viewpoints, which is hard to accomplish. Only when we are truly enlightened, will our thoughts and viewpoints be correct. Before we reach enlightenment, we can adopt the proper thoughts and viewpoints of Buddha Shakyamuni as ours. All the thoughts and viewpoints within the sutras are correct. We can at first rely on Buddha Shakyamuni, but only for a while, as he does not want us to rely upon him forever. This is like a student relying on teachers in school but becoming independent after graduation. Likewise, before we attain great enlightenment, we need to rely on Buddha Shakyamuni and Buddha Amitabha as our teachers.

Where is the Buddha? The Buddha is within the sutras, as Buddha Shakyamuni stated in the <u>Infinite Sutra</u> and Buddha

Amitabha relayed to us through the Forty-eight Great Vows. Relying on the teachings within the sutra is relying on the Buddha. We would do well to practice earnestly what the Buddha taught us to do or refrain from doing. In this way we will be true and good students. Applying this concept in our daily living is to return and rely upon the Dharma Jewel.

The Sangha of the Sangha Jewel represents purity and harmony as in the Six Principles of Harmony. Consequently, whenever we see a monk and nun, we do not want to dwell on whether this person is a great cultivator or a violator of precepts. Whether they are or are not is not our concern. Seeing a monk or a nun reminds us to see whether we ourselves have lived by the Six Principles of Harmony, or have cultivated purity of mind. To truly take refuge is to know how to reflect on ourselves, since we still have all the same bad habits and are committing the same offenses, having been deluded for infinite eons.

It would be helpful for Buddhists to set up the Triple Jewels in their home. When we make offerings to the Buddha statue or picture, we will be reminded that we need to be awakened. How? When our six senses encounter the external environment, we would not discriminate or attach, or give rise to any thoughts. For example, meditation is not giving rise to any discriminating thoughts or attachments. Thus one achieves a high level of wisdom and is able to see all situations clearly. However, ordinary people like us, use the false mind and constantly give rise to wandering and discriminating thoughts and attachments in these situations. The appearance of everything we see is false. Once we have understood these principles and learned how to not have wandering thoughts and attachments, we can also become a Bodhisattva or Buddha.

Taking the Three Refuges is a beginning step in practicing Buddhism. From there, we proceed on to foundation of Theravada Buddhism then to Mahayana Buddhism for the Third Condition, which is comprised of:

(A) Generating the Bodhi mind,

(B) Deeply believing in the Law of Cause and Effect,

(C) Reciting and upholding Mahayana sutras and

(D) Encouraging others on the path to Enlightenment.

Before practicing Mahayana Buddhism, we need to generate the Bodhi mind. Bodhi means awakening, thus, the Bodhi mind is an awakened mind. How will one be awakened? When one first realizes and understands that this world is full of sufferings.

Upon careful and rational observation of society, we may find our conclusions frightening. Looking back over the last thirty years, we see that people used to be kinder and more considerate. Whereas, people nowadays are more selfish and usually only think of benefiting oneself at the expense of others. This selfishness has created a chaotic world making even the climate abnormal. Therefore, the first thing in generating the Bodhi mind is to realize that this world is filled with sufferings and that the Western Pure Land is filled with bliss. True awakening is when one seeks to escape these sufferings then to attain happiness.

Second, awakening is the aspiration to benefit and help all sentient beings, to think of others and not of oneself. What are the urgent needs of sentient beings?

There is nothing more important than the Buddha's teachings. Thus, our most pressing need is nurturing and training lecturers to continue to pass on Buddhism. Today due to our advanced printing skills, numerous sutras have been distributed throughout the world, but regretfully, few people lecture on them. Since people have the tendency to misunderstand the meanings within the sutras, we need qualified people to lecture and explain them. Today the best way to benefit others is to train lecturers and at the same time gain innumerable merits. We work toward this goal with a great tolerant mind, not just for one Way Place, area or country but for the whole world. If only one country prospers and the others are poor, the poor will envy and resent the prosperous, leading to conflicts or worse. How could one pass the days peacefully knowing this? If everyone is prosperous, then all will be happy and peaceful.

Once there is a good number of lecturers to help others clearly understand the principles of the Buddha's teachings, they will in turn gradually help others in reaching awakening to break through delusion and escape suffering thus attaining happiness. This is the most beneficial way for one to put the Bodhi mind into practice.

To believe deeply in the Law of Cause and Effect does not simply refer to "What goes around comes around." The profound meaning is, "Being mindful of Buddha Amitabha is the cause and becoming Buddha is the consequence."

For the Pure Land practitioner, reciting and upholding Mahayana Sutras can be accomplished by reciting the Infinite Life Sutra. Delving deeply into one method can be achieved by concentrating on one sutra. If one does not think this is sufficient, the four other sutras and one commentary of the Pure Land School could also be recited. These six are more than enough. Simply allow them to take root and flourish. Finally, one encourages others on the path to enlightenment. The first three parts of the Third Condition benefit the self. The last one teaches us to dedicate the benefits we have received to all others; to help them to understand, practice and succeed in their cultivation of Buddhism. When attaining achievement in the Buddha's teachings, one succeeds in attaining infinite wisdom.

The Six Harmonies

The Three Conditions are the first of The Five Guidelines of the foundation for Pure Land practice. We have yet to become Buddhas or to depart from this world. Even when one becomes a Buddha, one does not leave all behind as

Buddhas want to help all sentient beings in the ten directions.

How does one get along with others harmoniously? The Buddha set six principles for us to follow. Not only are these applicable within a Buddhist community but also in all organizations or groups. When we take refuge in the Triple Jewels, there is a saying, "To return and rely upon the Sangha, the most worthy of respect of all groups." Group means a gathering of people. In our society, the smallest group of people is a family, a larger one is a nation and the largest is the union of many nations. Actually, the whole world is a group of which we all are a part. Why is a Buddhist community the most precious of all groups? The six rules that the Buddha set for Buddhist communities are something all its members follow, making this group the most worthy of respect and of being a role model for all.

The first of the Six Principles of Harmony is to share the same goals and viewpoints, in other words to establish a common consensus. Everyone within this group shares similar thoughts and viewpoints, providing the foundation for living in harmony. If everyone has different viewpoints and ideas, then conflicts would be unavoidable, making the group discordant. Therefore, sharing the same goals and viewpoints is very important, making this the first of the Six Principles.

The second of the Principles is to observe the same precepts and rules. There are both broad and narrow meanings within the word "Precept." The narrow meaning includes upholding the five or ten layperson precepts, monk's or nun's precepts, or Bodhisattva precepts and the Buddha's teachings. In a broader sense, "Observing precepts" includes abiding by etiquette, customs, rules and laws of the entire world.

Today, through the advancement of technology in travel and communication, our sphere of activity is not limited to our country but expands to other countries as well. Whether sightseeing, on business, or visiting others, it is essential to observe the local customs and laws, to live in harmony, thus being welcomed and respected by others. This principle is practical and brings joy to others; therefore, upholding Buddhist precepts also includes following the customs and laws of the country. All governments welcome law-abiding citizens, so to truly promote and be a benefactor of Buddhism is to uphold the precepts. With this as a base, people could then harmoniously live without arguments and share the joy of practicing together. When living together and sharing a common consensus, a group would naturally not have any conflicts. To practice with the same goal and to achieve improvement daily would ensure that the community would experience joy and inner peace.

The last of the Six Principles is to share benefits equally. Benefits refer to our daily necessities. A Sangha does not merely represent a community of monks and nuns. At home, the family can also practice Buddhism and accord with the Six Principles of Harmony to make up a sangha. Even within a company, everyone, from the employer to the workers, can practice Buddhism to make up a sangha. Therefore, sangha has a very broad meaning. Within a Sangha, one strives to share benefits. For left-home people it means having the same manner of living, from the abbot to one with no formal responsibilities within the community, everyone shares the same manner of living, with no special treatment. We would do well to live by the Six Principles of Harmony to learn how to better get along with others. When with other organizations or groups, regardless of whether or not they follow the Six Principles of Harmony, we ourselves need to accord with the spirit of these Principles to truly follow the Buddha's teachings.

Buddhas and Bodhisattvas are our best role models while we are to be good role models for others who are not Buddhists. This is the spirit of Buddhism, using our own behavior to influence and benefit others, thus promoting Buddhism. We do not teach others in the formal sense but simply let them observe us. Thus our daily conduct and practice can unobtrusively and imperceptibly help to influence and change others like Buddhas or Bodhisattvas manifesting in this world to teach sentient beings.

The Three Learnings

The third guideline is the Three Learnings: discipline, concentration and wisdom. The Three Learnings summarize all the teachings from Buddha Shakyamuni and all the Buddhas in the past, present and future. The Great Canon of Sutras is divided into three sections: sutras, vinaya or precepts, and sastras or commentaries. Sutras include the teachings of meditation, vinaya includes the teachings of discipline or precepts, sastra includes the teachings of wisdom. These Three Learnings of discipline, concentration and meditation represent the core of the Buddha's teachings.

The teachings of precepts place most emphasis on rules, regulations and laws. The earth has four seasonal changes: spring, summer, autumn and winter. We need rules and laws to successfully interact with people and matters, thus enabling the members of society to enjoy a wonderful and fulfilling life. A world absent of law and order is a world of chaos. Although one may possess good fortune and wealth, one may still be unhappy, living in fear and insecurity. Why? We have discarded law and order. The precepts thoroughly explain the principles, methods and the level of mind we need to bring about law and order. The Three Learnings clearly explain this concept. We practice the Buddha's teachings in order to attain the ultimate, perfect wisdom. Once we uncover this inner wisdom, we will know the true reality of life and the universe, including how to restore our original abilities.

The Buddha told us that all sentient beings possess a Buddha's wisdom and virtuous abilities. While the knowledge of the past, present and future is part of our original ability, they are unfortunately covered and hidden by our delusion. Delusion occurs when the mind/heart is not still, while an enlightened one remains unaffected. When our six senses encounter the environment, our mind/heart moves, giving rise to wandering thoughts.

The Buddha taught numerous ways to practice so we can remain unaffected in all situations, not giving rise to any wandering, discriminating thoughts or attachments, thus recovering our original capabilities. This state of mind is deep concentration. Cultivation is correcting one's erroneous thoughts, speech and behavior. What are the standards for these? They are discipline and concentration. Discipline is the external standard and precept observation is the internal standard; concentration is the standard for the pure mind. The external standard is very important, but much more important is the internal standard, because it helps us to achieve our goal in the practice to attain wisdom.

With discipline, we attain the concentration that gives rise to wisdom. This ultimate, perfect wisdom is called "Annuttara-Samyak-Sambodhi." How does one first attain proper realization, then equal and proper realization, and finally perfect, complete realization? These levels of attainment depend on the strength of concentration, the extent of the purity of mind. As Buddhists, the goal of our practice is Perfect, Complete Enlightenment. If one departs from rules of order and purity of mind, one is not practicing Buddhism. No matter which method one practices, whether Buddha Name Chanting, precept observing, mantra chanting, or Zen meditation; if one does not follow the guidelines, one cannot attain the pure mind. All would be just window dressing. With one degree of pure mind, we attain one degree of wisdom. With two degrees of pure mind, we attain two degrees of wisdom, etc. Therefore, practicing accordingly and maintaining and protecting the pure mind, which gives rise to true wisdom, is exceptionally important.

The Six Paramitas or Principles

The fourth guideline is the Six Principles or Paramitas that are the primary living principles of Bodhisattvas. Each principle encompasses our whole way of living; for example, the first of the Six Principles is "Giving." Some people think of giving as simply donating money. Actually, this is only one of the infinite kinds of giving. From the appearance, giving is sacrificing oneself to give to others. However, from its intrinsic nature, giving is letting go.

We can practice giving of our wealth or physical strength. For example, a homemaker keeps house daily providing a comfortable environment for the family. Without proper understanding, this homemaker may feel these daily chores are repetitive; that washing clothes and cooking meals are boring. If however, the homemaker clearly understands that he or she is cultivating the Bodhisattva Way by practicing the Six Principles, then he or she will be filled with joy. Changing one's perception of doing the same chores with a giving, non-attaching heart is practicing the principle of giving. Not only does one serve the whole family by keeping the house neat, but one also serves as a role model for all relatives and neighbors. In this way, not just one but all beings benefit. One is thus a family role model for all families. Whether managing a store or business, being a role model for others is practicing the Bodhisattva Way in guiding sentient beings. The principle of giving can be expanded to the infinite universe and beyond. With this extensive broad-mindedness, one is a Mahayana Bodhisattva.

Giving is comprised of three categories: wealth, teaching and fearlessness. The giving of wealth includes internal and external wealth. Internal wealth involves all of our mental and physical labors that benefit others. External wealth is the giving of all other things, e.g. money, food, etc. Gaining wealth is the result of giving wealth. The giving of teaching is the willingness to instruct others while not selfishly holding back any knowledge. It is to do one's best in educating willing students. As a result, one gains intelligence and wisdom. The giving of fearlessness includes soothing away other's fears and providing a feeling of security. As a result, one gains health and long life. Most people wish for wealth, intelligence, wisdom, health and long life. When there is a good cause, a good reward will follow. One does not receive a reward without first planting the good cause. By practicing all three kinds of giving, one perfectly attains all these rewards.

Observing carefully, we will see that there are not many who have all they wish for. Some wealthy employers do not possess great intelligence or wisdom, but have intelligent and wise employees working under them, following their instructions. These intelligent and wise employees have cultivated wisdom in their past lives but did not cultivate good fortune. On the other hand, these employers cultivated good fortune but did not cultivate wisdom. Cause and effect may be complex, but not hard to distinguish. Thus, using Buddhist principles to observe society enables one to know how to conduct oneself in the future.

In reality, true wisdom is more important than good fortune. Wealth is good fortune, but how one uses and allocates wealth requires a high level of wisdom. Without wisdom, possessing wealth may lead one to create infinite bad karma from bad deeds, thinking one is doing good. Without wisdom, one is unable to distinguish true from false, proper from deviated, right from wrong or beneficial from harmful. Often one is ignorant of having conducted oneself in an erroneous manner.

All these principles are explained very clearly in <u>Liao Fan's Four Lessons</u>. Within good and bad there exists true and false, half and full, right and wrong. From its appearance, what may appear to be a true good deed, due to changes in its nature some time later, can turn out to have been a bad one. On the other hand, what may initially appear to be a bad deed can turn out to have been a good one. Therefore, one needs insight to understand the outcome of all good and bad deeds and not to judge them by their initial appearance. One needs a high level of wisdom to understand deeply and to be far-sighted enough to distinguish correctly the truth.

The second principle is "Precept Observation," which also has a broad meaning. One follows the Buddha's teachings, accords with the customs of society, and abides by the rules and laws of a country. In both the spirit of the law as well as the letter, all rules and laws need to be followed.

The third principle is "Patience." Patience includes long-term patience whether interacting with people, matters or objects. As the Buddha explained in the <u>Diamond Sutra</u>, all dharma is attained from patience and endurance. To succeed in either worldly or spiritual dharma, one must have patience. Without it one cannot attain achievement. Having this patience to endure what others cannot, one achieves what others cannot. Only then will one accomplish great deeds.

The fourth principle is "Diligence." Diligence is seeking focused improvement daily, not trying to advance in many different directions. Advancing with diligence to a certain level, one attains concentration. This concentration does not simply mean cultivating while sitting in a lotus position facing a wall. It is to have a firm hold of one's mind and not to be influenced by external conditions. This accords with the Diamond Sutra, to remain unmoved by and unattached to any phenomenon. Not attaching to any phenomenon is to not be enticed by temptations from external influences. One achieves concentration when one is unmoved by all phenomena, such as the advancement of scientific technology, so confusing yet dazzling to our eyes. It is seeing everything clearly and knowing that all is intuitive wisdom, the prajna wisdom. In this way, one will then live happily.

For example, when we buy a refrigerator, use and maintain it nicely, it can last at least ten years. During these ten years, there will be improvements and changes in refrigerator manufacturing. Will we want to exchange it for a new one? When there is no need for a new one and we continue to use it, we have concentration. When we are moved upon seeing a new model in the store and want to buy it to replace the old one, afraid that guests will laugh at the latter's appearance; we have neither concentration nor wisdom. Living in this way, one would not be happy because one's income would slip through one's fingers just trying to keep up with new products. Buddhism calls this Mara, what comes to make one suffer, in this case, to tempt one to spend all their hard-earned money. A truly wise person would be unmoved and live a happy fulfilling life without worries or afflictions, unlike ordinary people.

The Ten Great Vows of
Universal Worthy Bodhisattva

The fifth and last of the guidelines is the Ten Great Vows of Universal Worthy Bodhisattva. Universal Worthy Bodhisattva is unlike any other Bodhisattva due to his great broadmindedness, where his every thought is of helping all sentient beings. He does not think of himself, his family, country or world but of the infinite universe and beyond, reaching true perfection. With this great broad mind, all that he practices is great.

The order in practicing Buddhism is belief, understanding, practice and attainment. First, one needs to have unwavering belief, for without it one is unable to accept the Buddha's teachings. It is not that easy to instill this belief, as it depends on affinity or condition. In Buddhism, these conditions include good roots, good fortune, merits, virtues and cause. Without these, it would be extremely difficult to have this unwavering belief. In believing, one needs to first believe that one possesses the Buddha nature and that one can definitely become a Buddha. Second, we need to have confidence in our original teacher, Buddha Shakyamuni, knowing that he would not lie to us. We also need to believe that what the great masters and Patriarchs have passed down to us is truthful. However, simply believing is not enough.

Equally important is that one seeks the

correct and perfect understanding. After understanding, one needs to accomplish, to practice, to apply Buddhist principles, methods and levels of attainment into one's daily living. Lastly, the attainment is to prove within our daily lives that all the teachings and understandings are correct.

Lately, I have heard some fellow practitioners mention that lacking a blessing from an Esoteric Master would seem to make one inferior to others. In reality, are these kinds of blessing all that effective? In America, many fellow practitioners were so enthusiastic about this ritual that they would even drive ten hours or more just to find a Master to obtain a consecration. After they came back, I asked them if they had uncovered their wisdom and had fewer afflictions. They honestly shook their heads and said no. I said, if a consecration is achieved by sprinkling a few drops of water on the head, then one might as well go take a shower to receive a great consecration.

Not understanding the true characteristics and meanings behind all the rituals reveals a very sad phenomenon in Buddhism. Mr. Nian-Chu Huang who was an Esoteric master, stated very clearly in his commentary of the <u>Infinite Life Sutra,</u> "The consecration is a blessing of compassion and kindness; one's head symbolizes the act of instilling in the person the outstanding teachings of the Buddha."

Chapter Five: The Pure Land School

Today, as we practice the Pure Land method, we know that the <u>Infinite Life Sutra</u> is a very important sutra, thus is a supreme Dharma. Passing on the <u>Infinite Life Sutra</u> and the <u>Amitabha Sutra</u> to others brings them a great consecration. Reciting the sutra once is to receive consecration once from all the Buddhas in the ten directions. Reciting the sutra twice is to receive consecration twice from all the Buddhas. Therefore, one needs to understand the method in practicing, to start from the foundation of the Three Conditions.

As I said earlier, the first condition is to be filial and respectful toward parents and teachers; to be compassionate and not kill any living being; and to cultivate the Ten Good Conducts. Cultivation begins from here. If one thinks that one cannot accomplish the above, then no matter how one practices, it is only superficial. It is important for one to practice earnestly to accomplish these conditions or one may not attain the true benefits from the Buddha's teachings.

Ultimately, we return to the Pure Land method. Why? To return to the Pure Land method is what all Buddhas recommend we do. In the <u>Amitabha Sutra</u>, all the Buddhas in the six directions praise the Pure Land. In the <u>Infinite Life Sutra</u>, Buddha Shakyamuni was very clear in praising Buddha Amitabha as the most respected, with the brightest of light, the king of all Buddhas. When returning to and relying upon a Buddha, who would be better than the best? Buddha Shakyamuni did not ask us to return and rely upon himself but rather upon Buddha Amitabha, for he is the ultimate Buddha of all Buddhas.

In the <u>Flower Adornment Sutra,</u> we see

that both Manjusri and Universal Worthy Bodhisattvas sought birth into the Western Pure Land. If the Western Pure Land were not so remarkable, why would these two Bodhisattvas of the Hwa Dzan world want to go to this particular Pure Land? The Infinite Life Sutra explains why one would want to chant Buddha Amitabha's name and be born into the Pure Land. If one would recite the Infinite Life Sutra more often and listen to lectures on it, one would come to a deeper and more meaningful understanding and cultivation.

If we do not wish to spend more time and energy to seek the truth of life and the universe, then following the teachings within this sutra would be sufficient and perfect. Why? In the future, after we are born into the Pure Land, our wisdom, virtuous abilities and enjoyments will be equal to those of Buddha Amitabha. We will then clearly understand the truth of life and the universe. Thus, as ancient wise people often said, the Pure Land method is a short cut to the ultimate Enlightenment.

Using other methods, we take a long circuitous route to achieve Enlightenment. Seeking birth into the Pure Land is the short cut that ensures us of attaining Enlightenment in one lifetime. From this, we know that this method is outstanding and beyond comparison. All Buddhas, Bodhisattvas and past Patriarchs have praised this method. It is a rare opportunity for us to encounter it in this lifetime. As is said in the opening verse of the sutras, "Difficult to encounter in infinite eons." Having encountered it in this lifetime, it would be unbearably sad to let this rarest of opportunities pass us by. It occurs so infrequently in infinite eons, we need to hold on tight, to not let go, to learn and practice as earnestly and sincerely as we can.

THE
THREE
REFUGES

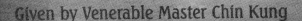

Given by Venerable Master Chin Kung

The Three Refuges

Table of Contents

"Taking Refuge in the Triple Jewels"
Singapore 1992

Dear fellow practitioners, today we are going to conduct the Initiation Ceremony of the Triple Jewels, which are the Buddha, the Dharma and the Sangha. I would like to clarify what taking refuge in the Triple Jewels means since there have been growing misunderstandings in modern times. In order to reap the true benefits, we must first settle these misunderstandings.

What is Buddhism? Is it a religion? Buddhism is not a religion but rather the most profound and wholesome education based on forty-nine years of Buddha Shakyamuni's teachings for all sentient beings. As I recall, in 1923, Mr. Chin-wu O-Yung spoke at the University of Zhong-Shan. The title of his lecture was "Buddhism is Neither a Religion, nor a Philosophy, but the Essential of the Modern World." This lecture was an insightful breakthrough that shook the contemporary Chinese Buddhist world.

Since Buddhism is an education, what exactly are its objectives, methods and principles? Its educational objective is to help sentient beings understand the truth of the Dharma which is defined as (1) the teachings of the Buddhas (2) duties, laws and doctrines or (3) things, events, phenomena, everything. Simply put, the truth of the Dharma addresses the causes that initiate all the phenomena of life and the universe. Life refers to ourselves while the universe refers to our living environment. Therefore, the educational content of Buddhism directs us to gain clear understanding of our living environment and ourselves.

Nowadays, the formal educational system only subscribes to a partial understanding of the universe, which has yet to be proven. Moreover, we are still discussing and investigating this limited part, not yet knowing enough to draw the correct conclusions. Unfortunately, even religions cannot provide comprehensive and satisfactory explanations of life as a whole, and are only confined to a limited area of the truth. Therefore, the profound and extensive educational content of Buddhism is essential for every sentient being.

The boundary of our living space is not restricted to a city, a region or even just the planet earth. There are galaxies in outer space, comprised of innumerable planets, on which exist advanced life forms that are much more intelligent than human beings. All these galaxies are also our living environment. Furthermore, apart from the space dimension, there is also a time dimension, which extends from the past through the present and into the future. Thus, the environment in which we live consists of an infinite magnitude of space and time.

Our current formal education does not cover such an extensive discussion of this infinite living space and time. Even the well-respected Confucianism only involves a single lifetime, ranging from birth to death and ultimately to a strong relationship that links us to our ancestors. The teachings of Confucius barely touch on the heavenly beings or ghosts but instead focus on how to behave as an honorable person. In contrast, Buddha Shakyamuni clearly and precisely described the Four Sage Realms, which are Buddha, Bodhisattva, Pratyekabuddha and Sound-hearer. Apart from the Four Sage Realms are the Six Realms of Reincarnation of heavenly beings, Asuras, humans, animals, hungry ghosts and hells. Levels of awakening rank these Four Sage Realms and the Six Realms. For example, Buddhas have the most awakened minds while beings in the hells have the most deluded minds. By combining the Six Realms and the Four Sage Realms, we have the Ten Realms. These comprise our existing living space and it is essential for us to clearly understand them.

After we understand the truth of life and the universe, our thoughts, viewpoints, speech and be-

4

havior would naturally differ from before. In the past, our deluded mind and erroneous viewpoints led to incorrect actions, thereby creating bad karma, which is the future retribution resulting from one's thoughts, speech and action. According to the fundamental Law of Cause and Effect, unavoidable consequences will result from creating karma, as good results come from good karma and bad results come from bad karma. One creates one's own destiny; no one can step in to bear the consequences of our actions.

As we can see, thoroughly understanding the truth of life and the universe will bring us infinite benefits. Once we understand and deeply believe in the Law of Cause and Effect, we will not create any more bad karma. If we do not create any more karma, then we will not have to bear the consequences or fruits, thus achieving what the Buddha frequently referred to in the sutras as surpassing the Ten Realms. From the Cause and Effect point of view, the Four Sage Realms are the results of diligent cultivation and attainment, while the Six

Realms are the consequences of good or bad deeds. The Six Realms can be further categorized into the Three Good Realms of humans, Asuras and heavenly beings and the Three Bad Realms of hells, hungry ghosts and animals.

After understanding karma and its consequences, we will refrain from creating any more karma or at least not any bad ones. By applying the above concepts to our daily lives, we will obtain what everyone wishes for: a happy life, pleasant family, successful career, harmonious society, prosperous nation and peaceful world. Only the Buddha's education completely provides the solution to humanity's search for true happiness. Clearly understanding this, we realize that this education is essential for everyone. Since this education encompasses infinite space and time, it surpasses differences in nationality, race, political affiliation and religion. In other words, it is for all sentient beings in the Nine Realms below that of Buddhas.

There are several examples in the sutras about different religious followers who learned the Buddha's teachings during Buddha Shakyamuni's time. The <u>Flower Adornment Sutra</u> and the <u>Earth Store Sutra</u>, tell respectively of a Hindu priest and a daughter of a Hindu priest who, by adhering to the Buddha's teaching have attained the level of Bodhisattva. From these examples, we understand that the Buddha's education indeed transcends religious beliefs and that any religious followers can benefit from it.

The educational system founded by the Buddha is similar to our contemporary educational system. For example, becoming an Arhat is equivalent to earning a University Bachelor's degree and becoming a Bodhisattva is equivalent to earning a Master's degree. Buddhahood, the highest degree, is equivalent to a Ph.D. Followers of any religion can attain these stages of enlightenment. Is it necessary to abandon one's religion and learn the Buddha's education to obtain enlightenment? Definitely not. If one were to go to school or study abroad to pursue knowledge and advancement, one need not change nationality or religion. In other words, the purpose of studying does not conflict with nationality, religion, etc.

Therefore, Buddhism is an education. Titles such as Arhat, Bodhisattva and Buddha are nothing but "degree" names. Regardless of our differences, we shall achieve these degrees equally as long as we diligently follow the teachings. Thus, the Initiation Ceremony of the Triple Jewels is to formally enroll one into a school where Buddha Shakyamuni teaches the objective, methods and principles of attaining enlightenment.

Since Buddha Shakyamuni established Buddhism, we acknowledge him as our original teacher. Actually, there is only one teacher, Buddha Shakyamuni, for all Buddhists. Bodhisattvas such as Manjusri (symbolizing wisdom), Samantabhadra (symbolizing great vows) and Avalokiteshvara (symbolizing compassion) were all the

Buddha's earlier students. Today, we too are the Buddha's students. These Bodhisattvas are our schoolmates, seniors who studied before us while we are freshmen. As they are seniors and have the ability to teach us, Buddhas, Bodhisattvas and Arhats are not objects for worship but rather someone we can respect and learn from.

What is the ultimate goal of the Buddha's education? The sutras teach us that it is Anuttara-Samyak-Sambodhi. This very important and well-respected phrase is transliterated from Sanskrit in order to keep its original pronunciation. It means the highest, proper and complete enlightenment. Simply said, it can be interpreted as the ultimate, perfect wisdom. Whoever obtains it will be able to intuitively know and sense every aspect of the true reality of life and the universe. Obtaining this wisdom and ability is the ultimate goal of all the Buddha's students.

The Buddha teaches us that the ultimate perfect wisdom is innate. The <u>Avatamsaka (Flower Adornment) Sutra</u> states, "Every being possesses the same wisdom and virtuous capabilities as Buddhas." Why do we not have this wisdom now? It is because of "wandering thoughts and attachments." This statement clearly reveals the two causes of how we temporarily have lost our original capabilities. Wandering thoughts and attachments are not within our basic nature; therefore, they can be discarded. Like dispersing the clouds to let the sun shine through, we remove wandering thoughts and attachments from our mind and cultivate virtue to restore our Buddha Nature, thus completely recovering our innate abilities.

In practice, how do we cultivate? Formally taking refuge in the Triple Jewels is the initial step as it symbolizes asking Venerables, monks or nuns, to pass on ways of Buddhist cultivation. Taking Refuge means to find a shelter that we can return to and rely on or what Buddhists call "Return to the other shore." In practice, from where do we return and upon what do we rely? We return to and rely upon the Triple Jewels of the Buddha, the Dharma and the Sangha.

In the first step, we return to and rely on the Buddha. "Buddha" is a Sanskrit word meaning awareness and understanding. When we take refuge in the Buddha, we are returning from our deluded state of mind and relying upon an awakened, understanding mind. Participating in the Initiation Ceremony and accepting the Buddha's teachings are the first steps of the awakening in becoming aware of the importance of learning his education.

The Sixth Patriarch of Zen, Master Hui-Neng, used a different approach in explaining the Triple Jewels. He did not use the words "Buddha, Dharma and Sangha" for fear of promoting misconceptions in the Triple Jewels for future generations. He was afraid that as Buddhism was passed from generation to generation, if he used these words, people would form erroneous views, automatically thinking of a statue for the Buddha Jewel, a sutra for the Dharma Jewel and a Buddhist monk or nun for the Sangha Jewel. These are not what we should return to. Actually, we should take refuge in our Self-Nature Buddha. A Bodhisattva stated, "The Self-Nature Awareness is innate." Therefore, what Buddha Shakyamuni meant in taking refuge in the Buddha is not to seek protection under his wing, but to return from our delusive mind and rely upon the innate Self-Nature Buddha. It is essential for one to understand the importance of returning to one's Self-Nature.

In the second step, we take refuge in the Dharma, returning from deviant views by relying upon proper views and understanding. Dharma is the proper comprehension and viewpoint of life and the universe. The Dharma Jewel is the infinite, innate wisdom of Self-Nature also referred to as the Prajna Wisdom. Relying upon our Prajna Wisdom to correct our erroneous thoughts, speech and behavior is the meaning of taking refuge in the Dharma Jewel. Among the Three Jewels, the

Dharma is the primary one we should rely on. In this day and age, Prajna Wisdom will be our primary concern.

However, our innate wisdom cannot be restored in a short time. Then what should we follow? Sutras are records of the Buddha's teachings that describe the truth of the universe. Before our Prajna Wisdom has been fully recovered, we follow the teachings in the sutras and use them as a guideline. If our thinking coincides with the sutras, then our comprehension is correct. For example, the Buddha teaches us to respect and take care of our parents and teachers, to be compassionate by not killing and to practice the Ten Good Conducts. People may wonder in this modern age why we should be following what the Buddha taught three thousand years ago. We do so because the Self-Nature Prajna Wisdom is everlasting and unchanged; those who obtain it have the capability to know everything in the past, present and future within the infinite universe.

However, we must beware of fraudulent sutras. It is easy for us to encounter fake sutras, especially in a modern world that promotes freedom of publication. Essentially anyone can publish books. In ancient times when sutras first came to China, each sutra had to undergo a strict examination by experts, followed by the emperor's official seal to prove its authenticity. Even the sutra commentaries of ancient patriarchs underwent scrutiny from highly accomplished monks and scholars of that time before receiving the Emperor's approval for distribution. Nowadays, no one regulates or enforces this process. Therefore, we need to be careful in verifying the authenticity of a sutra by checking for its listing in the Dragon (Chien-Long) Canon of the Sutras. This Canon of thirty-eight volumes was compiled under the decree of Emperor Chien-Long in 1738. Previous canons were meticulously certified by the most accomplished monks and scholars of their time and thus also serve as reliable references.

In the third step, we take refuge in the Sangha Jewel. Used here, Sangha does not mean a group of monks or nuns. There are two representations, purity of mind and harmony in life. First, Sangha refers to living in a way that keeps our minds far away from temptations while maintaining the purity of our six senses of sight, sound, taste, smell, touch and mind object. In the modern world, people suffer from pollution of mind, spirit and body. Even the earth's ecological system is off-balance. There are holes in the ozone layers that are "pollution" of the skies. Almost everything from the skies and the earth to their inhabitants are contaminated in one way or another. Today, everyone is aware of environmental pollution. Governments are also promoting environmental protection to ensure better living conditions. However, how effective are these protection programs? It is questionable. The problem comes back to what the Buddha revealed, that the environment, the dependent variable, changes with our minds, the independent variable. If the impurities in our mind cannot be eradicated, our environment will never reach a state of purity. Therefore, if we want to improve the external environment, we first start internally by purifying our mind. Taking refuge in the third Jewel, the Sangha, thus means returning from pollution and relying upon purity of mind.

Second, the Sangha represents harmony in living. Having observed the sufferings resulting from the disharmony between peoples, countries and even religions, the Buddha taught us the Six Principles of Harmony. The Six Principles are the essential guidelines that all Buddhists need to observe. When we take refuge in the Sangha, we are returning from pollution and disharmony and relying upon Purity of Mind and the Six Principles of Harmony. Thus, the guidelines for cultivation are:

(1)   Taking refuge in the Buddha - awareness without delusion,

(2)   Taking refuge in the Dharma - proper viewpoints without deviation,

16

(3)   Taking refuge in the Sangha - purity without pollution.

These are the primary disciplines in practicing Buddhism from the beginning of cultivation to the attainment of Buddhahood.

The main purpose behind taking the Three Refuges is to cultivate practicing awakening, proper thoughts and viewpoints, and purity. From now on, if people ask us what we are cultivating, we can answer that we are cultivating the Three Refuges. What are we learning? We are learning to achieve the ultimate, perfect wisdom that comes from perfecting these Three Refuges. What are the methods we use for cultivation? There are innumerable methods available depending on the ability and condition of each individual practitioner. Methods are not fixed, but flexible. However, we must remember that our learning objective always remains the same; awakening, proper thoughts and viewpoints, and purity.

For Pure Land practitioners, the main cultivation method we use is chanting Buddha Amitabha's name. This method is advocated by Mahasthamaprapta (Great Strength) Bodhisattva in the <u>Surangama Sutra</u> and by Samantabhadra (Universal Worthy) Bodhisattva in the <u>Avatamsaka (Flower Adornment) Sutra</u>.

In addition to chanting Buddha Amitabha's name, we follow the Five Guidelines to help us in our daily cultivation. First, we advocate Confucius' Five Virtues of Gentility, Kindness, Respectfulness, Thriftiness and Humility. We use these Five Virtues to cultivate our body and mind. Practicing them provides the foundation for our cultivation. The first level is comprised of the Three Conditions that are described in the <u>Visualization Sutra</u>. The First Condition includes (a) being filial and respectful to one's parents and teachers, (b) being compassionate and not killing any living beings and (c) practicing the Ten Good Conducts. The second Condition includes (a) following the Three Refuges, (b) observing precepts,

18

laws and customs and (c) behaving in a proper and dignified manner. The Third Condition includes (a) generating our Bodhi-Mind, (b) deeply believing in the Law of Cause and Effect, (c) reciting and upholding Mahayana Sutras and (d) encouraging others to advance on the path to Enlightenment. The Buddha told us that the Three Conditions are the causes that brought all the Buddhas of the three times and the ten directions to Enlightenment. Therefore, we cannot do without this important step in our practice.

Proceeding upward from the Three Conditions, we advance to the second level which is the Six Principles of Harmony. The First Principle of Harmony is to share the same viewpoints or goals. There will be no conflict in the world if we all share the same thoughts and viewpoints. This principle tries to create a common understanding for all sentient beings. This common understanding is based on our Self-Nature and not on Buddha Shakyamuni's opinion. He taught us how to cultivate and explore our own innate wisdom, virtues and capabilities. We are not imitating him; rather we are rediscovering our inborn potential. His education is truly extraordinary.

The second principle is to observe the same precepts. Practicing the precepts includes cultivating an attitude of following society's laws and customs. Once everyone shares the common viewpoints and is able to follow the law, society will be peaceful and prosperous and world peace will naturally ensue.

Another important principle is to share benefits equally. In modern society, it is beneficial not to have a big difference in wealth between people but to try to close the gap between the "have's" and the "have-nots." Equal sharing of wealth consequently settles the conflicts over wealth. Sharing benefits equally with others is a deed of wisdom and a real cultivation of good fortune. The reason people do not have equal wealth comes from the different seeds that they have previously planted.

If people did not plant the same seeds, how can they expect to harvest the same fruits? The Buddha taught that those who harvest more should share with those who harvest less. Then, the sharing behavior becomes the seeds that will benefit one more later. According to the Law of Cause and Effect, poor people need to cultivate more good fortune to receive better harvests in the future. In addition, the wealthy need to share their possessions in order to remain wealthy in the future. Only by doing so will the world become peaceful. This true merit comes from learning the Buddha's teachings.

Pure Land practitioners, as a foundation, cultivate the Confucian Five Virtues that are basic for all humanity. From here, we advance to the Three Conditions and the Six Principles of Harmony that are the important basis before practicing Buddhism. Then the Three Learnings are the foundation before practicing Mahayana Buddhism that includes the Six Paramitas. Finally, we practice the Ten Great Vows of Samantabhadra (Universal

Worthy) Bodhisattva to attain Buddhahood. It is not difficult to remember these five guidelines. Combining this solid foundation with chanting Buddha Amitabha's name will assure us of obtaining what people have always pursued, a harmonious family life, a successful career and a peaceful society. Now that we have a clear understanding of what we are learning and sincerely want to follow the teachings, we need to practice diligently toward accomplishing our ideal goal. Consequently, one returns and relies on one's Triple Jewels of Self-Nature.

In addition to the abstract form of the Triple Jewels of Self-Nature, there are the physical forms seen as Buddha's images, sutras, monks and nuns. Making offerings to the Buddha's image serves two purposes. First, it honors our original teacher, Buddha Shakyamuni. Every time we look at the image, we remember the great teachings he passed on to us. Second, it is to remind us to emulate the Buddha. When we see the Buddha's image, we remind ourselves to strive for awakening and not to be deluded. Sutras serve the same purpose by reminding us that we have taken refuge in the Dharma and need to reflect upon our viewpoints and comprehension. Similarly, seeing a monk or nun, representing the Sangha, can remind us of the importance of maintaining purity of the six senses and harmony with others. Therefore, attending the physical form of the Triple Jewels greatly benefits us because they constantly remind us of the path to awakening.

Some practitioners attend the physical forms of the Triple Jewels at home. The Buddha's image symbolizes the Buddha Jewel while the Bodhisattva's image represents the Sangha Jewel. When we honor the Three Sages of the Western Pure Land, Buddha Amitabha symbolizes the Buddha Jewel, and Avalokiteshvara and Mahasthamaprapta Bodhisattvas symbolize the Sangha Jewel. Furthermore, Buddhist sutras symbolize the Dharma Jewel. These three remind us of the treasures of Self-Nature within us.

Of all the Buddhist sutras, the <u>Infinite Life Sutra</u> is what I recommend the most. Although not too lengthy, the text completely encompasses the Buddha's teachings. Thus, it is well suited to modern practitioners. The full title of this sutra is <u>The Buddha Speaks of the Infinite Life Sutra of Adornment, Purity, Equality and Enlightenment of the Mahayana School.</u> This title fully reveals the objectives, principles and methods of cultivation in the Buddha's teachings. "Infinite Life" in this sutra's title embodies the most important of all the other infinities, including infinite wisdom, abilities, virtues, wealth, etc. Without infinite life, one could not enjoy all these other infinities. The infinity of our natural potential is what Pure Land practitioners seek and the virtues and capabilities of our innate Self-Nature are infinite. Furthermore, infinite Dharma originates from Self-Nature. Thus, the immeasurable unbounded existences of the Ten Realms are created by the Self-Nature.

The word "Adornment" in the sutra's title represents truth, goodness, beauty and wisdom, qualities that are not a true reality in this world. They exist within the Self-Nature and will be found when one seeks within.

The principles of cultivation are also expressed by "Purity, Equality and Enlightenment." Purity represents the Buddha Jewel; Equality represents the Dharma Jewel; and Enlightenment represents the Buddha Jewel. These three concepts are also equivalent to the Three Learnings, and cover the Buddha's forty-nine years of teachings. Purity stands for self-discipline and the Vinayas (Precepts); Equality stands for the Concentration and the Sutras; Enlightenment stands for the Wisdom and the Sastras (Commentaries).

If we have a busy lifestyle and do not have time to study numerous Buddhist sutras, we can start from this <u>Infinite Life Sutra</u>. Once thoroughly understanding it, not only will one understand Buddha Shakyamuni's teachings but also the teachings of all the Buddhas, because all these teachings come from the Self-Nature.

The Buddha Speaks of the Infinite Life Sutra of Adornment, Purity, Equality, and Enlightenment of the Mahayana School expresses the essence of all sutras. Practicing according to the teachings in this sutra fulfills the requirements of taking refuge in the Triple Jewels!

Today, I have explained to everyone the meaning of taking the Three Refuges. We will begin the Three Refuges Ceremony by sincerely and respectfully repeating the oath three times in front of the Buddha, vowing to be willing to become Buddha's student and to learn from him. I, Venerable Chin-Kung, will be the witness and initiation teacher. Please remember that one does not take refuge in the monk conducting the ceremony, but rather in the Buddha, the Dharma and the Sangha, thus becoming students of the Triple Jewels.

The following is a simple yet solemn initiation ceremony. Everyone will receive a certificate of the initiation with an oath extracted from the <u>Book of the Precepts</u> by Dharma Master Hong-I. We use it for commemoration and simplicity. Let us stand in front of the Buddha's and Bodhisattva's images with our most sincere, pure, compassionate and respectful heart. Repeat after me, "I solemnly pledge to be a student of the Triple Jewels. From now on, I will cultivate according to the Buddha's teachings, will seek rebirth into the Pure Land and will help all other sentient beings to understand the truth of the Dharma."

What is Taking Refuge?

Taking Refuge means to return and rely. From where do we return from and upon what do we rely? When we take refuge in the Buddha, we are returning from our deluded state of mind and relying upon an Awakened, Understanding mind. When we take refuge in the Dharma, we are returning from deviant views and relying upon proper views and understanding. When we take refuge in the Sangha, we are returning from pollution and disharmony and relying upon Purity of Mind and the Six Principles of Harmony. Taking refuge in the Triple Jewels restores the complete wisdom and abilities of our Self-Nature. We will attain purity, equality, honesty, contentment, compassion and overall, true happiness.

The Buddha Jewel

Buddha is a Sanskrit word meaning Awareness and Understanding. When we take refuge in the Buddha, we vow to return from blind faith and delusion and rely upon Understanding and Awareness as a way of life. We are not relying upon the statues or Buddha-images, but rather the spirit of understanding and awareness they represent.

As students of the Pure Land Teachings, we learn to rely upon Buddha Amitabha's lessons on wisdom and compassion. The name "Amitabha" stands for Infinite Light and Infinite Life. When we follow his teachings, we will attain wisdom, happiness and longevity.

This is taking refuge in the Buddha.

The Dharma Jewel

Dharma means Right Understanding and Views. Delusion has obstructed us from seeing the true face of people and the reality behind matters and objects. This has caused us to look at life and the universe in a distorted and deviant way. When delusion is cleared and our minds are pure to an extent, we give rise to wisdom. With wisdom, we are able to see all people and matters completely and clearly. When our hearts are pure, we can see the past, present and future. Only when we have clearly seen the whole can our viewpoint and understanding be considered right.

The Buddha's mind is pure without the slightest pollution and therefore sees everything clearly and entirely. We can rely upon the sutras, which are the recorded teachings of the Buddha, because they speak entirely of the truths the Buddha has seen. They teach and show us the way to attain Purity of Mind, to see life and the universe most clearly and become just like the Buddhas.

As students of the Pure Land Teachings, we should rely upon the five Sutras and one commentary of the Pure Land as guidelines of practice:

1. <u>The Buddha Speaks of the Infinite Life Sutra of Adornment, Purity, Equality and Enlightenment of the Mahayana School</u>

2. <u>The Amitabha Sutra</u>

3. <u>The Visualization Sutra</u>

4. "The Chapter of Universal Worthy Bodhisattva's Conduct and Vows "

5. "The Chapter on the Foremost Attainment of Great Strength Bodhisattva through Buddha Recitation "

6. "Vasubandhu Bodhisattva's Report on the Way to Reaching the Pure Land "

This is taking refuge in the Dharma.

The Sangha Jewel

Sangha means purity and harmony. Today's world is full of pollution; pollution of mind, spirit, views and body. Even the earth and atmosphere are hazardly polluted. The Buddha taught, "The environment changes according to our state of mind." We would do well to return from all these pollutants and rely upon Purity of Mind, for it is the key to saving our Earth.

There is also great disharmony in our world today, among spouses, families, friends, societies and countries which has brought us much suffering and many disasters. The Buddha taught us to rely upon the Six Principles of Living in Harmony to establish harmonious relationships between others and ourselves.

As students of the Pure Land Teachings, we rely upon wisdom and compassion as our way of treating others and dealing with affairs. Great Strength Bodhisattva represents wisdom. His choice of the Buddha Recitation method of practice is wisdom in its highest form. Guan Yin Bodhisattva represents compassion; when we help introduce the Pure Land Teachings to others, we are practicing the compassion of Guan Yin Bodhisattva.

This is taking refuge in the Sangha.

To the Buddha I return and rely,
returning from delusions and
relying upon Awareness and Understanding.

To the Dharma I return and rely,
returning from erroneous views and
relying upon Proper Views and
Understanding.

To the Sangha I return and rely,
returning from pollution and disharmony and
relying upon Purity of Mind and the
Six Principles of Harmony.

Pure Mind
Quiet Heart

Volume One

Venerable Master Chin Kung

Remember the

Kindness of Others:

Repay the Kindness

with Gratitude

Pure Mind,
Quiet Heart

Contents

Part One:
Pure Mind
Quiet Heart

True Sincerity
Towards Others

❀ The foundation of our practice is based on the great compassionate mind, the sincere and true mind, the Bodhi Mind. It is the mind of benefiting all sentient beings.

❀ If we have one degree of sincerity within, the Buddhas and Bodhisattvas will help us one degree. Two degrees of sincerity and they will help us two degrees, etc.

❀ To listen to a dharma talk is to practice self-discipline, deep concentration and wisdom. After sincerely doing so for three to five years we will achieve. If we understand intuitively, we will truly understand. If we understand by thinking, we will not.

❀ Master Yin Guang said that everything is attained

from sincerity and respect. Sincerity is benefiting
oneself; respect is benefiting others.

❀ With sincerity and respect, we will be in harmony
with others.

❀ A good way place cannot be established without
good external conditions, which come from good
inner conditions. To have good inner conditions we
need to generate the mind of sincerity to bring the
Dharma to all sentient beings. There must be no
desire to benefit self. Trivial selfishness will block the
response from Buddhas and Bodhisattvas.

❀ Where do we start our practice? Think only of others, not of oneself.

❀ If we can accept all karmic creditors as having
been our parents in former lifetimes who will become Buddhas in a future lifetime, we will regard
them very differently, without fear or anger. Can

you start from this point? If yes, then doubt can be replaced by belief.

❀ The ancient sages told us to practice humility to reduce the arrogance that we have accumulated over uncountable lifetimes.

❀ Respect every being, matter and phenomenon.

❀ To benefit others is good. To benefit oneself is bad.

❀ Seek to benefit all sentient beings not just those like ourselves.

❀ Worldly people look at the facade. Wise people look at the inner beauty that is compassion, truthfulness and purity.

❀ Reflect on our past bad habits. This can help us to know what is good or bad.

❀ Remember the kindness of others: repay the debt with gratitude.

❀ Every thought for others is good. Every thought for ourselves is bad. How many of each have we had?

❀ Not being filial to others plants the seed to be born into the hell realm.

❀ We would do well to regard all others as Buddhas and Bodhisattvas who wish to help us.

❀ To benefit others is to benefit oneself.

Purity
of Mind within

❀ Why do I keep repeating the same things? Because you are still here. If you really understood you would have left for the Pure Land.

❀ What is cultivation? True cultivation is when we cultivate purity of mind even when we are in the most impure of environments. It is to practice patience and diligence even when we are in the most unendurable situations we may encounter.

❀ Always think of a person's good qualities, not their bad ones. This will help us to achieve good fortune and purity of mind thus gradually reducing our afflictions and wandering thoughts. If we are always thinking of the bad qualities of others, then we will be mired in the downward spiral of regression.

❀ Do all that is good, do nothing that is bad, maintain

purity of mind.

❀ If we have pure water but taint it with one drop of poison, all of the water becomes polluted. Likewise if we taint ourselves with wandering and discriminating thoughts, we will become polluted. Then there can be no response from the Buddhas.

❀ The pure mind has no discrimination or attachments.

❀ Think of others and the mind is pure. Think of self and the mind is polluted.

❀ To protect and purify the environment, we protect and purify our heart.

❀ Our good fortune, capability and wisdom are complete; none of them can be obtained externally. The Buddha teaches us to look for them within our mind, our pure mind.

❊ External conditions change with our heart. A mind of beauty will see only beauty. A mind of evil will see only evil. With true wisdom we will see only beauty.

❊ When we take refuge in the Buddha, we are returning from our deluded state of mind and relying upon an Awakened, Understanding mind. When we take refuge in the Dharma, we are returning from deviant views and relying upon proper views and understanding. When we take refuge in the Sangha, we are returning from pollution and disharmony and relying upon Purity of Mind and the Six Principles of Harmony.

Equality

In Everything We See

❀ Most people think disasters are natural, having nothing to do with us. However, the environment is a reflection of our mind. As our minds give rise to more thoughts of greed, anger, ignorance and inequality we have more disasters due to floods, fires, wind and earthquakes, respectively. The only way to change this is for people to reduce and eliminate these thoughts.

❀ There is no true or false in the Dharma. Everything is equal.

❀ Harmonious sharing of benefits.

❀ All methods of practice are equal.

❀ When we attain the mind of equality, we will attain deep concentration. Thus our inner nature, our true nature will be uncovered. This is the true treasure.

❀ When one thought of anger arises all the doors of obstacles will open and we will lose all our merits. Patience and tolerance will help us to retain these merits. However, anger will not result in losing our good fortune, which we can enjoy in the heaven, human and animal realms.

❀ The universe is one entity; if one part suffers and knows pain then we too suffer and know pain.

❀ The reason people do not have equal wealth comes from the different seeds that they have previously planted. If people did not plant the same seeds, how can they expect to harvest the same fruits?

❀ Most sentient beings have the seed of Buddha's teaching in their Alaya consciousness.

Proper Understanding
of Ourselves

❁ Do not be joyful when a bad person is about to be born into the Hell realm for this means that we have no loving-kindness. Instead, try to help them to turn back by understanding what they did in their greed and jealousy.

❁ We practice giving to end greed, follow the precepts to end bad karma, patience to end anger, diligence to end idleness, concentration to end scattered thoughts and wisdom to end ignorance.

❁ Of the three bad karmas, speech is the most damaging, the most serious and the easiest to commit. Feeling remorse can reduce the effect.

❁ Although it is hard to truly understand Buddhism, if we try diligently, we will do so and thus receive the benefits. However, if we merely study Buddhism, we will miss this rarest of opportunities.

❀ Understanding is to understand the principle. Practice is to feel remorse for our faults.

❀ To be close to the Teacher is to truly understand and follow what is taught. It is not being next to him or her every day.

❀ Why can we not fully understand? We are unable to abandon former improper viewpoints.

❀ Whether we accumulate merits or generate karmic results lies in one thought. Delusion at the time of that one thought creates karmic retribution.

❀ Understand that we have an affinity with all people we encounter. Once we understand this we will be able to accept the true reality that all have been our parents and all will become Buddhas. With this awareness everything else will come naturally and easily.

❀ To genuinely understand one sutra is to understand all sutras.

❀ We now have this rarest of opportunities to learn Buddhism. The question is whether we truly understand. If we do not firmly grasp on to it then misery and suffering lie ahead of us.

❀ If we do not know and understand the past as well as the present, we cannot help others.

❀ Understanding everything around us, without emotion, is deep concentration. This is the way to change the afflicted mind into the Bodhi Mind.

❀ After understanding karma and its consequences, we will refrain from creating any more karma or at least not any bad ones.

Compassion
Helping Others in A Wise and
Unconditional Way

❀ The great compassionate and sincere Bodhi Mind means to offer without selfishness. It is a mind without self-regard. It is a mind with no expectation of reward.

❀ We need to stop benefiting ourselves at the expense of hurting others for such behavior only creates bad karma that we will have to repay later. If we do not believe this it will still happen. To correct it, we need to constantly practice great compassion.

❀ We should never abandon anyone, if we can do nothing else, chant "Amitabha" to plant the seed. This is the great compassion.

❀ When we are treated with anger treat others with

compassion.

❀ When we attain the broad, compassionate heart we will break our ego attachment and thus become more patient.

❀ If we can treat everyone with compassion, we will live the life of Buddhas and Bodhisattvas.

❀ There is a big difference between love and compassion. Love comes from feelings; compassion comes from wisdom. Love is unstable and unreliable. We may love someone today but not tomorrow. When someone tells us that he or she loves or hates us, we would do well not to take it too seriously. However, compassion is for forever because it is based on the wisdom that is part of the true mind, our original self.

❀ If we constantly practice kindness, bad seeds will not be able to grow.

❀ If we constantly think about ourselves, the Buddhas cannot help us.

❀ Think of this body as a transformation body, to be used as Buddhas and Bodhisattvas would use one to help others.

❀ Can ordinary beings with heavy karma be helped? Yes, by correcting improper thoughts, speech and behavior.

❀ It is easiest to help those in the human realm because they are most capable of being awakened. But it still depends on affinity and condition.

❀ Even a Buddha cannot help those who are void of remorse.

❀ We cannot give up on any person.

❀ It is our responsibility to care for all beings because

we are all one entity. There is no why to it. Only confused and deluded beings ask why.

* We need to care for all beings as we care for our family. When they suffer, we suffer. When they are happy, we are happy.

* Our compassion for others should be equal without discrimination.

See Through
to the Truth of Impermanence

❀ When we understand the true reality, we will see
through and thus be able to let go. This letting go
will then enable us to better see through.

❀ Do not be affected or tempted by external conditions. We can listen and see but are to remain unmoved, our mind in stillness.

❀ When we first see an object, that first look is from
the true mind. That first look contains no discrimination, no attachment and no rising thought. With
that first look we see the nature of the objects outer
appearance. However, this time of true sight is less
that one-thousandth of a second. Immediately, the
second thought arises containing discrimination
and attachment.

❀ We are deluded as in a dream.

❀ A good friend can see the future and advise properly. A bad friend can only see the present, giving bad advice.

❀ The question is not whether our self-nature exists, but whether we are able to see it.

❀ The crucial question in the cycle of birth and death is where will we go after we die? Ahead of us are the ten realms. Which way will we go?

❀ As we can see, thoroughly understanding the truth of life and the universe will bring us infinite benefits. Once we understand and deeply believe in the Law of Cause and Effect, we will not create any more bad karma. If we do not create any more karma, then we will not have to bear the consequences or fruits.

❀ Obstacles are created by ourselves and thus need to be eradicated by ourselves.

Let Go
of All Wandering Thoughts and
Attachments

❀ What I read yesterday was wonderful, but what I read today was even more wonderful. I had to abandon yesterday's reading to take in today's. This is non-attachment. We attain and let go at the same time.

❀ To begin our practice we let go of all wandering and discriminating thoughts and attachments.

❀ The chaos and turmoil in the world today arise from our delusions, attachments and the Three Poisons of greed, anger and ignorance.

❀ If we work very hard and attach to the work, we are attaching to existence.

❀ All beings still mired in the six realms are attached to

something; hell beings to anger, hungry ghosts to greed and animals to ignorance.

❀ To begin to "Let go" we practice giving for six years. All the Buddhas and Bodhisattvas practice giving.

❀ Cultivation is reforming one's imperfections.

❀ Remember the "Four Universal Vows of Buddhas and Bodhisattvas".
  1. Sentient beings are innumerable,
     I vow to help them all,
  2. Afflictions are inexhaustible,
     I vow to end them all,
  3. Ways to practice are boundless,
     I vow to master them all and
  4. Enlightenment is unsurpassable,
     I vow to attain it.

❀ Giving without wisdom only results in more greed, in our wanting to gain more. This only brings us good fortune. Instead, we need to give to sever our greed. This brings us merits and virtues.

❀ Wealth comes from the giving of wealth; intelligence comes from the giving of teaching; health and long life come from the giving of fearlessness.

❀ Only question how we treat others, not how others treat us. Let go of the thought of their treatment of us.

❀ When we first cultivate, we will have sickness and pain, which arise from the Three Poisons of greed, anger and ignorance. But these will disappear. If we eliminate the Three Poisons, the external circumstances will reflect this change.

❀ The Buddha told us that if a sentient being cries then we cry. If a sentient being laughs then we laugh. However, we attach to neither the sadness nor to the joy.

22

* Greed, anger, ignorance, arrogance and doubt are the basis of our afflictions.

* We are not still here in the cycle of birth and death because the Buddha abandoned us, but rather because we have not yet truly accepted his teachings. We will leave when we can finally let go.

Attain Freedom
of Mind and Spirit

❀ All sickness comes from pollution and the worst pollution is that of the mind. The Buddha called this pollution the Three Poisons of greed, anger and ignorance. Between the pollution of the environment and that of our mind how can we not get sick? However, even with the worst pollution around us, a person who is free of the three Poisons will not get sick.

❀ Listen without listening. Do without doing.

❀ To see our faults is to be enlightened. To correct our faults is to practice.

❀ The cultivator who is truly happy has savored the Dharma joy. If not, something is wrong with their practice, not the teaching. A true cultivator is happy all day.

* Recite until the brightness within shines from our face.

* A moment without awakening is a moment with regression.

* Everything is empty and merely a dream. There is nothing to seek for all is unreal, merely illusion.

* We need to follow rules naturally, not forcing ourselves. This is the way of infinite brightness.

* Existence is like a cloud. From a distance it appears real. But when we pass through it, it is nothing.

* Emptiness is form; form is emptiness. Our self-nature is form and thus is emptiness.

* The mind encompasses the whole universe. The mind encompasses all the Buddhalands.

❁ All of life is just one entity with no beginning and no end.

❁ Taking refuge in the Triple Jewels restores the complete wisdom and abilities of our Self-Nature. We will attain purity, equality, honesty, contentment, compassion and overall, true happiness.

Accord with Conditions
Go Along With The
Environment

* Act willingly to accord with adversity. To dissolve our debts we need to repay them with calmness and serenity, with no hatred or grievance within our hearts. If we retain hatred within our heart, then the debt of the next lifetime will be much greater than it was in this one.

* We do not accord with conditions when we react from emotion. When we instead react from wisdom, our vows are very firm.

* When interacting with people, matters and affairs accord with conditions.

* You cannot force confidence in the Teacher; it depends on affinity.

❀ Go along with conditions do not seek them. In this way obstacles will be reduced.

❀ The accumulation of merit comes from according with conditions.

❀ If we are unmoved by a situation, then regardless of the circumstances, it is a good situation.

❀ If we are destined to have something, do not worry, we will receive it. But if we are not destined to have something then regardless of what we do we will not be able to hold on to it.

❀ Buddhas and Bodhisattvas transform according to what sentient beings need.

❀ True wisdom comes from deep concentration for with concentration we will have calmness and not be tempted by external phenomena.

Be Mindful Of
Buddha Amitabha
Following His Teachings and
Vowing To Reach the Pure Land.

❀ To practice the Buddha's teachings is to know great joy.

❀ Moving within the cycle of birth and death is to be in the Sea of Suffering. Our head comes out of the water for just a breath and then we sink once again.

❀ As ordinary people we still need the Buddha's teaching but once we cross the Sea of Suffering we leave behind the boat of the teachings.

❀ We have encountered innumerable Buddhas over infinite lifetimes. Then why are we still mired in this Saha world? Buddhas cannot help us until our conditions have matured.

◈ Buddhas and Bodhisattvas can show us the way, but we have to take it for ourselves.

◈ The Buddha taught us three basic principles. From precept observation we attain deep concentration. From deep concentration we attain wisdom. This is the way to attain supreme, perfect wisdom.

◈ If our "Amitabha" karma is heaviest, we will be born into the Pure Land. If our bad karma is heaviest, we will be born into the three bad realms.

◈ Buddha name chanting and sutra recitation are ways to obtain a response from Buddhas and Bodhisattvas.

◈ How do we gain wisdom? Many people who grew up in our modern society would say that wisdom is gained from information or knowledge. The Buddha told us the opposite! He taught us that wisdom is already within our self-nature; it does not come from the outside.

❋ It is a rare opportunity to encounter Buddhism. The hindrance to this is the selfishness that has been accumulated over infinite lifetimes and which is very strong.

❋ Our first hindrance to enlightenment is ego, our self-attachment, our every thought of ourselves. The Buddha said we have to have no-ego, no self.

Part Two:
Questions and
Answers

What is the purpose of being born?

We are born to repay or collect a debt, repay or collect kindness.

Can we take on the suffering of others?

No, karmic effects can only be endured or enjoyed by the individual, who created them, no one can take on another's karma.

Why does it take so long to attain achievement?

Attainment takes numerous eons because when we are not practicing we are regressing. As the opening verse to the sutras says, it takes infinite eons to encounter Buddhism. Then we have to first make up lost ground.

How do I know how much merit I have?

To know how much we can just think of when we last

became angry or even just irritated. Feeling either of these will destroy all that we have accumulated. Feeling arrogance will likewise destroy our merits. However, good fortune cannot be destroyed by these feelings.

How do I know if the method I have chosen is right for me?

Those who have the strength from cultivation are perfectly filled with dharma joy. If we feel miserable instead of joyful then the method we have chosen may not be suitable for us.

I have heard that we can stay in one realm due to attachment. Is this true?

One day Buddha Shakyamuni smiled, shook his head, pointed to a trail of ants on the ground and told his followers, "These ants have been reincarnated as ants for as long a time as seven Buddhas have appeared to teach. Why are they unable to change their form to be born into another realm? They are attached to their present forms."

What is a good student-teacher relationship?
A good student respects the Teacher. A good Teacher cares for the student as a child.

What is the self-nature?
The self-nature is our original, true self that we still have, but that is currently covered by deluded thoughts.

Why do you say feeling ashamed is helpful?
When we feel ashamed we will become more diligent.

Why is filial piety so important?
The practice of Filial Piety is showing respect and car-

ing for one's parents. The Chinese character "Shiao" means filial piety. The top part means old age while the bottom part means son. When the two are put together, it gives us the meaning of one entity. It is vastly expansive and never-ending. It speaks of the generations before ours and of those to follow.

What if we see faults in others?
The Sixth Patriarch of Zen, Master Hui Neng said that first we should not see the faults of others. Second we should not speak of the faults of others.

I have made so many mistakes in my life, how can I hope to achieve?

We have all made mistakes, we all have faults. Even equal enlightenment Bodhisattvas who are only one degree away from Buddhahood have made mistakes and have faults. What matters is to know and correct them until we have no more. Then we will reach

Buddhahood. Only Buddhas have no mistakes.

How do we achieve? Where do we begin?
Becoming Buddhas and Bodhisattvas is simply returning to our already perfect self-nature. First, we start by expanding our mind. A sign of delusion is being narrow-minded. When we expand our mind to care for all beings we are on the path to Buddhahood. If not, then we are still mired in the path of reincarnation.

Pure Mind,
Quiet Heart

Volume Two

Venerable Master Chin Kung

Translated by Silent Voices

Part One:
Pure Mind,
Quiet Heart

True Sincerity
Towards Others

❀ The self-nature is our true treasure. How do we uncover it? Through sincerity and respect.

❀ How can you tell if someone is an awakened being? They have no selfishness.

❀ We respect all beings, but we only praise those who are virtuous and thus worthy of praise.

❀ All the teachings of the Buddhas can be condensed into one word "Giving".

❀ Giving when no one knows that we have given is to gain great fortune.

❀ We need to not simply treat all others as parents and future Buddhas, but rather to make them our parents. As filial piety and respect are fundamental to our self-nature practicing in this manner will help us to uncover this self-nature.

❀ To practice is to change our bad habits. For, example, gossiping about others. These bad habits do not just harm us, but harm others as well. Changing ourselves for the benefit of others will make it easier to change.

❀ What is sincerity? No single thought arising.

❀ A good teacher is considerate, careful and compassionate to those who sincerely wish to work diligently to learn.

❀ The key in our cultivation is to generate the Bodhi heart, the great compassionate heart to care for and help all sentient beings. But this is not enough. We also need to treat all with the mind of sincerity, to treat all with filial respect.

Purity
of Mind Within

❋ Do not irritate others, become embroiled in disagreements or allow any conflict to continue.

❋ Deep concentration is not being attached to external forms. It is to remain in stillness and serenity.

❋ Originally, we were Buddhas. But now we are deluded and have temporarily lost our original self-nature, our original Buddha-nature.

❋ If we can correct just one fault every day for three years, we will become virtuous and achieve a higher level of awakening.

❋ What is the difference between ordinary people and Bodhisattvas? Bodhisattvas correct their faults every day until they become Buddhas. Ordinary people do not yet realize their faults.

❋ If our minds are pure, compassionate and kind, we will never encounter illness or disaster.

❀ We would do well to stay away from crowded and noisy places because they give rise to obstacles that disrupt our purity of mind.

❀ We start our practice from the still mind, the mind of tranquility, the mind of purity.

❀ Mara is something that comes to torture us, to interfere with our practice. How many of us can resist? How many of us can remain unaffected? Only by practicing self-discipline, deep concentration and wisdom can we remain unaffected.

❀ When we are mindful of the Buddha, with every thought to benefit others, we are Buddhas for that moment. When we are mindful of Mara, with every thought to benefit ourselves, we are Maras for that moment.

❀ Read the newspaper, listen to the television only for work-related information. Let go of everything else. It is all illusion, all unreal. Only purity of mind is real.

❀ If we do not wish to be affected by others or circumstances, we would do well to practice purity of mind. Purity of mind is to remain in the stillness, the state of no wandering

5

thoughts.

❀ Awakened beings see with wisdom eyes, the eyes of purity, equality and awakening. Ordinary people like us see with human eyes, the eyes of emotion that give rise to love and hatred.

❀ Our mind needs to remain in serenity. Our body needs to continue in movement.

❀ When our mind is at its purest we will recover our innate abilities and be able to hear the quietest sounds and see the least visible light.

Equality
in Everything We See

* If we still think of right and wrong, then we still have discrimination.

* Ignorance and understanding, life and death, good karma and bad karma all teach awakened beings. Because they have no discrimination awakened beings understand that everything is equal.

* If people are willing to accept teachings and we do not teach, our result will be ignorance.

* Everything is formed by a harmonious combination of elements.

* In Buddhism, all beings will become a Buddha but in religion, not all people will become a god.

* Different people need different teaching methods. All people are equal because they have the same self-nature. All methods are equal because they all lead to the same goal of enlightenment.

* All phenomena come from our self-nature.

Since our self-nature is equal, everything is equal. Once we understand this, we will no longer discriminate.

❀ Buddhism is an education, not a religion. When this is understood, then this education will be accepted by religions.

❀ True wisdom comes from purity, stillness, tranquility and concentration within, not from listening to different teachings, practicing different methods or reading many sutras.

Proper Understanding
of Ourselves

❀ To want to practice and learn successfully we need three affinities. First, our most important affinity is with our Teacher who provides constant guidance. Our next is with our fellow practitioners who provide encouragement. The third is with our way place, which provides the proper environment for our practice and learning.

❀ Our true understanding is like lighting a candle in a cave that has been dark for a thousand years. One candle illuminates the entire cave. The darkness symbolizes our ignorance. We commit wrongdoings because we are deluded. The candle symbolizes understanding the truth of life and the universe. So even though we have committed wrongdoings, once we understand we will become enlightened.

❀ 'No thought' means having 'no improper thought', it does not mean having no 'awakened thought'.

❀ Although we may not cultivate perfectly, little by little the merits that will be accumulated will be considerable.

❀ When we are in a good situation and start to feel proud of it we become arrogant. Arrogance is one of our major afflictions following greed, anger and ignorance.

❀ When we get along with others and practice the Giving of Fearlessness we will live long and healthy lives.

❀ We would do well to not immerse ourselves in greed, anger and ignorance but to engage our moral character, which flows from our self-nature.

❀ If we have a kind and gentle heart we will have a kind and gentle appearance.

❀ We all want to accumulate merits and virtues. Giving is to cultivate them and patience is to keep them. If we are not patient but give rise to resentment and anger we will constantly be burning up our merits and virtues.

❀ If people say they understand the teachings, but cannot put them into practice, they do not truly understand them.

❀ We would do well not to think of the wrongdoings we have committed, but feel remorse and vow to never commit them again. In thinking of the wrongdoing again, we again plant the seed in our Alaya Consciousness, which is the store consciousness, the thought database from all our past and present lives, good or bad.

❀ How do we begin our practice? Start with being filial to and caring for our parents. This is a crucial step in our attainment of Buddhahood. The teachings tell us that all sentient beings have been our parents and all will become future Buddhas.

❀ The Buddha told us that the happiness we experience when our unhappiness stops is only temporary. The happiness, which is permanent, comes from understanding the true reality of life and the universe.

❀ When we let go of wandering and discriminating thoughts and attachments, we rid ourselves of these karmic obstacles. Then all of our wishes will come true.

❀ We cannot force something to happen or expect someone to do something when conditions have not yet matured.

Compassion
By Helping Others in A Wise, Unconditional and Unemotional Way

❀ What is goodness and kindness? When we give of ourselves for the benefit of others.

❀ The problem is not that awakened beings do not want to help. The problem is that we do not want to listen, to accept their guidance.

❀ What is great compassion? Expecting nothing when caring unconditionally for others.

❀ Do not give up on any single person. Maybe in the future he or she will not be deluded. At that time when conditions have matured, we can help him or her.

❀ The true purpose of giving is to help sentient beings awaken. We do not require any reason, we do so simply because we are all one entity.

❀ To get along with others, to manage matters and to accept objects, ordinary people use emotion. Awakened beings use wisdom.

❀ Most people think money is of utmost importance in accumulating merits. They are wrong because merits are self-discipline, deep concentration, wisdom and the compassionate mind of caring.

❀ How do we help others settle their heart? We explain the Law of Cause and Effect and help them to be mindful of Buddha Amitabha to settle their hearts in awakening and peace. When the heart of every person is gentle and at peace, the disasters in the world will reduce.

❀ When our mind is broad, although we give just a little we will gain great good fortune. But when our mind is narrow, although we give a lot we will gain little good fortune.

See Through
to The Truth of Impermanence

❀ The real, permanent truth arises from having seen our self-nature.

❀ The simpler the life, the happier the life.

❀ All phenomena change constantly but the true-nature remains unchanged.

❀ Neither be happy when things go our way nor unhappy when they do not. Everything changes, nothing is real.

❀ The strength of our good karma is weak. The strength of our bad karma is strong. Knowing that we reap what we sow what can we do? Stop committing bad deeds and only do good ones.

❀ Why do we not see any improvement in our practice? Our thoughts are too scattered because we do not understand the true reality and are affected by the external world.

❀ Everything is impermanent, nothing stays the same. For example, we are not the same people we were in yesterday's photograph. If

14

everything is changeable and nothing stays the same, why should we attach to it?

❀ Why do we have nightmares? Because our bad habits and bad deeds accumulated over infinite past lifetimes have planted seeds in our Alaya consciousness. These can arise even as we sleep.

❀ Giving dharma talks is a way to overcome our bad habits and afflictions, thus reducing our karmic obstacles. Lecturing everyday reminds us daily of the teachings.

❀ Observing precepts or self-discipline is knowing how to get along with people. Wisdom is to see through. Concentration is to let go. Practicing these will help us to understand that the true reality is neither existing nor empty.

❀ Only when our mind is in a state of serenity can we experience deep concentration. Only when our mind is in a state of deep concentration can we experience our original, innate wisdom.

❀ The true dharma joy is based on wisdom. It is the only true happiness that is permanent.

❀ Wealth is just like running water passing through. Remember that it is only illusion, not real.

Let Go of All Wandering
Thoughts and Attachments

❁ When we let go of our discrimination and attachment, we will see everything as one. Only then can our self-discipline, deep concentration and wisdom be complete. If we cannot accomplish this perfectly then maybe, we can at least achieve one percent.

❁ Whenever we sleep, we have dreams, which arise from our wandering thoughts.

❁ Wandering thoughts use up most of our energy. When we have less wandering thoughts, we will need less food.

❁ When we let go of our greed, anger and ignorance, our wisdom will arise.

❁ It is easy for awakened beings to help those whose conditions have matured. But those whose conditions have not yet matured are not ready to accept the teachings. However, we can create the opportunities to help them listen to more talks and have more opportunities to practice.

❁ Pure giving is when we have no attachment to

the thought that we have given, that someone
has received or that something has been given.

❀ The more time we spend with others the
more we concentrate on their bad habits
while neglecting their good points. When
people are too close, they may separate in the
future. To have a lasting relationship, maintain a suitable distance. We would also do
well to remember that the Buddha teaches us
not to see the faults of others.

❀ Although we intend to behave properly, for
example not to lose our temper, something
happens and we become angry before we can
stop ourselves. When we give rise to thoughts
of greed and do not get what we want, we
give way to resentment. This is because we
are controlled by our negative karma. Negative karma includes wandering thoughts, and
attachments, greed, anger, ignorance and arrogance. How do we overcome it? By listening more to lectures and putting these teachings into practice. Understanding and practice are equally important as they comple-
ment each other and lead to even higher understanding and practice.

❀ The more we attach the lower we fall in the

three bad realms of reincarnation.

❀ The key to success in our practice is to let go in our mind.

❀ When chanting we do not want to be attached to the thought of who is chanting or to what is being chanted.

❀ With even the smallest desire for fame or wealth, we cannot transcend the cycle of rein-carnation.

❀ Our biggest obstacle is arrogance. This comes from self-attachment, from egoism. To rid ourselves of arrogance we practice respect and humility.

❀ Our primary affliction is our attachment to our body.

❀ Buddha Shakyamuni severed the five desires of wealth, lust, fame, food/drink and sleep to achieve the state of serenity. We think he sac-rificed. He simply let go.

❀ Whether we attach to thought or to no thought, we are still attached.

❀ Cultivating a non-discriminating mind provides the serenity for practitioners to let go of afflictions, wandering thoughts and attachments. It is difficult for most of us to let go due to the injustices we feel we have suffered and the grudges we thus hold. However, feeling this way only puts us at more of a disadvantage because then we suffer the consequences of our grudges. Inequalities exist in this world because of our discriminating mind.

Attain Freedom
of Mind and Spirit

❀ If we do not practice, but simply study; we just become Buddhist scholars.

❀ When we do not have enough time to mind ourselves, how do we have the time to mind others?

❀ I have awakened you 10,000 times but still you sleep! If you can listen and take this into your heart, then you are rare indeed.

❀ Our fear and worry over death arise from our strong attachment to our body.

❀ True happiness is not the comfortable or luxurious life that we are now enjoying. It is the contentment that can truly nurture our lives.

❀ Our lives should be like the strings of a lute. If the strings are too tight they will break. If they are too loose they will not play. They need to be balanced, as do we. This is to practice the middle way.

❀ Wandering thoughts and attachments are not

within our innate nature; therefore, they can be discarded.

❀ There are at least three kinds of karma. Good leads us to the upper three realms; bad leads us to the lower three realms. But there is also a third kind; pure karma that leads us to the Pure Land. Pure karma is created when we interact with others, matters and things with the mind of purity, equality and enlightenment.

❀ The Cultivation Hall is the best place to calm our mind.

❀ We need to change our greed, anger and ignorance to sharing the same viewpoints or goals, observing the same precepts, living and practicing together harmoniously, not quarrelling, experiencing the inner peace and happiness from practicing together and sharing benefits harmoniously. When we accomplish these, we will feel lighter, more at ease, happier and healthier. This will in turn transform our environment.

Accord with Conditions
to Go Along with the Environment

* We need to accord with people because this is the only way we can help them. As we do this we feel joyful over their accomplishments.

* When we encounter a situation with one who wishes us ill use wisdom to resolve it. If they wish to harm us remember that this is simply Cause and Effect at work. If we calmly accept the effect, this will end the negative affinity. Otherwise it will continue and become even more severe.

* Everything we encounter is affinity, everything is constantly changing.

* It is easier to form an animosity than to dissolve one. How do we do this? Willingly endure the consequences and do not get upset over them. We should instead feel gratitude for they have helped us to dissolve a karmic debt. This is true wisdom.

* Good roots mean understanding and achievement. Good fortune and virtues mean practice and achievement.

❀ In this world, when we do not get what we wish, it is because the thoughts and actions of our innumerable lifetimes have been improper.

❀ The merits of Buddhas are the same, only their affinities are different. The vows and affinities of Buddha Amitabha exceed those of other Buddhas. We also need to establish many Dharma affinities to help teach as many sentient beings as possible.

❀ Decreasing our greed, anger and ignorance and increasing our good roots is the foundation of all our achievements.

Be Mindful of Buddha Amitabha
Following His Teachings and Vowing To Reach the Pure Land.

* Both the seeking of good karma and the creating of bad karma keep us in the six realms. Good karma will result in our going to the three good realms and bad karma will result in our going to the three bad realms. Instead, we can accumulate pure karma from diligently doing kind deeds while not asking for any rewards. We can then dedicate the merits from these kind deeds to being born into the Pure Land.

* If we can let go of our greed, anger, ignorance, arrogance, doubt and improper viewpoints, we can transcend the cycle of birth and death. But when we once again desire something, the cycle again arises.

* When we know and understand the suffering of life, and believe, accept and practice the teachings, we can transcend the cycle of birth and death.

* We need good roots, good fortune, good affinity and virtue to encounter the proper teachings.

❁ Practice strengthens understanding. Understanding strengthens practice.

❁ When our thoughts are proper our body will return to its healthy state. How do we do this? By studying and practicing the Buddha's teachings, improper thoughts will be replaced by proper ones. This will then be reflected throughout the universe.

❁ In order to achieve we need to constantly observe ourselves and refrain from wrongdoing.

❁ When we adopt the vows of the *Earth Treasure Sutra*, we are Earth Treasure Bodhisattva. When we adopt the vows of Universal Worthy Bodhisattva, we are Universal Worthy Bodhisattva. When we adopt the vows of Buddha Amitabha, we are Buddha Amitabha.

❁ How long does it take to reach achievement? From history we know this can be accomplished in three years.

❁ Without the presence of filial piety, Buddhism cannot take root.

❁ Buddha Shakyamuni lived a simple life; one meal a day, three clothes, sleeping under a tree at night, yet he lived a happy, content life. By following his example and living a simple lifestyle we can reduce our attachments and likewise lead contented lives.

❀ A practitioner who cannot achieve concentration will not attain enlightenment. All they can do is just plant the seeds for future lifetimes.

❀ To achieve true understanding, use intuition not thought when listening to lectures. Do no attach to either the words or the speech.

❀ The mind at peace, the mind in stillness will help us to gain insight.

❀ If we cannot apply the principles to our daily lives we will not reach achievement. We will just become a Buddhist scholar.

❀ If we are awakened, we use our mind of wisdom. When not yet awakened we use our mind of delusion and our emotions.

❀ It is said that in the first year of our practice, the Buddha is right before our eyes. The second year he is in the distance. The third year he is as smoke in the air.

Part Two:
Questions and
Answers

We do not have a way place to cultivate in. Should we start one or if not how do we know when it is time to start one?

We can start a way place with our existing good fortune. But without a response from the Buddhas, when that good fortune runs out the way place will not survive. Do not be afraid of not having a way place. Instead, be afraid of not having diligent cultivators. Think carefully before building a way place. Is it really necessary? Are there enough cultivators?

With the compassion to help others, how do we establish an affinity with a way place?

When we enter the cultivation hall we can make three vows. First, I vow to establish an affinity with this way place, to help all those who are here. Second, I vow to establish an affinity with all those who live here. Third, I vow to establish an affinity with all those who practice here.

At times, I feel that life is overwhelming. What can I do?

Today, people have to take tranquilizers to be able to sleep. Why? They feel their lives are out of control. They wish to dominate other people and to possess more things. Fifty years ago, people had time to appreciate nature, time to study the works of wise people. Today we have no time for nature: no time for contemplation. We live a luxurious life compared to our predecessors but have no spiritual life. We search for excitement to paralyze our feelings. How can we fix this? Reduce our time at work, at play. With purity of mind, we will require less. Our lives are wasted in our attempts to attain things. We brought nothing into this life: we will take nothing when we leave it. What we need is a simple manner of living. Work one year; take off one year. A simple manner of living brings us happiness and serenity. If we do not attach to giving or receiving we will enter the awakened beings state of tranquility.

Why do I often see the lotus flower in Buddhist art?
We use the lotus flower to symbolize transcending the ten realms of existence. First, it rises through the mud at the bottom of the pond, which symbolizes the six realms of birth and death. Then, it rises through the water, which symbolizes the four sage realms. Finally, it breaks through the surface of the water completely transcending the ten realms, reaching the one true Dharma realm.

The lotus flower teaches us that although we live in the world, we should not become polluted by our surroundings. The lotus flower above the water symbolizes that one day, all beings, from those in the hell realms to those who are Bodhisattvas, will become Buddhas. The Buddha realm exceeds the ten realms and to become a Buddha is the ultimate goal of our teachings. So, when we see the lotus flower, we are reminded to practice the teachings and to transcend the ten realms. This is the meaning of the lotus flower and is why we see it so often.

Can different beings live in the same space?
Today science has advanced to the level where people have landed on the moon. The <u>Flower Adornment Sutra</u> tells of the Moon Prince. Is this true? After astronauts landed on the moon, some people asked, "Do we still chant the name of the Moon Prince? Is he real"? The Buddha told us there was a moon prince so yes we still chant. On earth, ghosts and humans live together in the same space but in different dimensions so they cannot see each other. What the Buddha taught we can prove in deep concentration. When our minds are pure we can enter that space.

Why do you say that being ashamed is good?
Lacking wisdom, we cannot break through discriminating and wandering thoughts. If we cannot break through then we are destined to be shameful. Others are in the Western Pure Land, why am I still here? This is the greatest shame. To be ashamed is to be able to change, to be able to achieve.

THE ART

OF

LIVING

**Selected Teachings of
Venerable Teacher Chin Kung**

TABLE OF CONTENTS

THE EDUCATION OF TEACHER SHAKYAMUNI

❖

"Education - The field of study
concerned with teaching and learning"
- THE AMERICAN HERITAGE DICTIONARY

Buddhism is an education about us, and our living environment. The Buddha teaches us to recognize ourselves; our thoughts, speech, and actions and the consequences they evoke. Most importantly, the Buddha wants us to restore our original and complete wisdom. He teaches that everyone possesses the ability to attain complete understanding of life and the universe, and it is only because of delusion that we are unable to realize it. We are blinded by wandering thoughts, discriminations, and attachments, and forget the original pure mind of our self nature. In this way, we have caused ourselves much unneeded suffering.

The Buddha also teaches us to view our environment clearly. 'Environment' refers to the people, matters, and objects we come across everyday. When our hearts are free from discriminations and attachments, we would be able to view everything clearly and deal with them appropriately. Thus, we can live in harmony with others and succeed in all our endeavours.

❖

What did the Buddha mean when he taught us to cultivate? His intent was none other than to rid us of our delusions and attachments. If we drew together the Six Principles of practice taught by the Buddha, we would only end up with the practice of giving. Giving simply means to let go. If we can let go of our greed, hatred, ignorance, and arrogance, then we would always dwell in purity of mind. If we can let go of all discriminations, worries, and attachments, then we would attain peace, freedom, health, and longevity. If we can let go of our own views and work together for the benefit of others, then we can achieve harmony with others, harmony in society, and ultimately, world peace. From this we can see that the main practice of the Buddha's teachings is none other than giving.

When the Teacher Shakyamuni was in the world, he not only used words to teach, but made an example of himself for all living beings to follow. He let go of all desires, worldly enjoyments, fame, and money to lead the life of a left-home monk. He lived a lifestyle of simplicity, purity of mind and body, and happiness. Mundane people would see this as bitter and pitiful, but this is only due to their deluded and upside-down views. One with wisdom would view things differently. The wise would see the Buddha's lifestyle as one of true freedom, happiness, and fulfilment. The Buddha does not have useless thoughts, discriminations, attachments, or worries. How at ease he is! He accords with all conditions and emanates wisdom in every thought, speech, and action to teach living beings in this world.

The Buddhas live lives of wisdom, while mundane people live lives of affliction. Shakyamuni's teachings teach us how to change afflicted lives into ones of great wisdom. From these teachers, we will learn how to restore the ultimate and complete wisdom and abilities of our self nature; allowing us to attain true happiness and prosperity. This, is the Buddha's Education.

THE 4 KINDS OF BUDDHISM TODAY

In our world today, there are at least four different types of Buddhism. The first type is the authentic Buddhism, the education of understanding the true face of life and the universe originally intended by Shakyamuni Buddha. Unfortunately, the authentic Buddha's education is rare nowadays, and difficult to encounter. The remaining types of Buddhism are more or less distortions of the original teachings.

The second type of Buddhism is the religious Buddhism. Originally, Buddhism was not a religion, but now it has become one. We can no longer deny that there is a 'Buddhist religion' because everywhere we look, Buddhism is displayed as a religion. Unlike the monasteries in the past which held eight-hour classes per day and provided another eight hours for self-cultivation, today's Buddhist 'temples' no longer uphold such a perseverance of the

Buddha's Teachings. Today we mainly see people offering to the Buddha statues and praying for blessings and fortune. In this way, Buddhism has been wrongly changed into a religion.

The third type of Buddhism is the philosophical study of the Buddha's teachings. Many universities today open courses on the study of Buddhist Sutras, considering the teachings as a philosophy. The content of the Buddha's education is actually a complete university of knowledge and wisdom. Philosophy is only one of its courses. Just as it is wrong to recognize an university as a single course, it is also inappropriate to think of and limit the Buddha's education as only a philosophy. The Buddha's education can help us resolve our problems - from family difficulties to the great issue of life and death. The Buddha's teachings are deep and vast, and teach us the truths of life and the universe. It should not be mistaken as only a philosophy.

The fourth type of Buddhism we see in our world today is the deviant and externalist Buddhism. This is an extremely unfortunate affair which only came to be in the past 30-40 years. We must know that the religious Buddhism persuades people to be descent, and the philosophical Buddhism pursues truth, neither cause much harm to the society. If Buddhism is changed into a deviant and externalist path, using the weakness of the human nature to cheat and harm living beings; disturbing the peace and safety of the society, then this conversion of Buddhism has gone too far. The speech and actions of these deviant and externalist paths can be very attractive and enticing. One should be very careful as not to be mislead by these deviant ways, or regretting it would be too late.

These four types of Buddhism exist in our society today, we should recognize them as they are and think carefully as to which way is most beneficial to us, and the one we will ultimately follow.

THE ART OF LIVING
– SELECTED PASSAGES –
HOUSTON 1996
TALK GIVEN BY THE VENERABLE CHIN KUNG

ೞ Our goal in studying Buddhism is to open up our wisdom; to attain this goal, we must cultivate purity of mind. In today's society, our greatest obstructions are TV, radio, newspapers, and magazines - these all contain contents which pollute our minds. I often persuade people not to read or listen to these things. When our hearts are free from these unneeded afflictions, we can live each day in peace and happiness; thus, allowing our minds to return to purity. With an undeluded mind, one will see matters of life clearer, deeper, and farther than others. This is because a settled and concentrated mind is a mind of wisdom. The key in cultivating the Buddha's teachings is having a settled and concentrated mind, in practicing the Pure Land method, purity of mind is of foremost importance.

ༀ The <u>Infinite Life Sutra</u> teaches us to cultivate purity, equality, and understanding. Being mindful of the Buddha is cultivating this, for Amitabha Buddha is purity, equality, and understanding. When we recite the Buddha's name, we are reminded of these qualities.

ༀ In China, Buddhism can be divided into ten schools. Aside from the two Small Vehicle school which has already declined, there are eight schools remaining belonging to Great Vehicle Buddhism. There are 2 schools (Ch'an and Shing) which enter the Buddha's teachings through the method of "Understanding/ Enlightenment". They seek the great enlightening, to understand the heart/mind, and see the self-nature. Usually, those of lesser capabilities to enlighten on their own are unable to reach their goals through this method. Thus, to cultivate the Ch'an/Zen School requires a high level of wisdom and a very pure heart. Without these, then one would have to start learning from the stage of Teachings. The study of Teachings is to help establish proper understanding and proper viewpoint, thus, the method of "Righteousness/ Properness" is used here to enter the Buddha's teachings. There are 4 schools belonging to this category (Tien Tai, Shian Shou, Fa Shiang, and San Lwun). The practitioners of these schools study and abide by the teachings of Shakyamuni Buddha to correct their erroneous views, thoughts, and actions. Most people are capable of learning this method, but it is a long journey, such as going to school. One must start from elementary school, then gradually advance grade by grade to junior high, high school, and college. In finishing one grade, one attains the benefit of that single grade. The final 2 schools are Pure Land and Esoteric. These stress on the importance of cultivating purity of mind, thus, their method of entering the Buddha's teachings is through "Purity". The Pure Land School can be practiced by people of all capabilities, regardless whether they be smart or dull. All can practice, and all can succeed in cultivating Pure Land. The Esoteric School requires a high level of Purity of Mind, making it very difficult to reach attainment.

ଔ The difference between the cultivation of Purity in Pure Land School and Esoteric School is that the Pure Land School teaches us to cultivate purity of mind away from pollution, while the Esoteric School teaches us to cultivate purity of mind in the midst of pollution, the latter path involves state of being in pollution but not being polluted; naturally, this state is too difficult for commonfolk to succeed in attaining.

ଔ True wisdom arises from purity of mind, thus, "wisdom" mentioned in the Buddha's teachings is not attained from reading and studying books; the "wisdom" we attain from reading and studying is only worldly knowledge, and not true wisdom.

ભ True wisdom is the function of our self-nature. Our self-nature is complete with unlimited wisdom, virtues, and abilities, these qualities are present in everyone's self-nature, and we must know to bring them out.

ભ 'Buddha' is Purity, Equality, and Understanding. The Buddha's teachings can be summarized into 10 simple phrases: **True Sincerity** towards others, **Purity of Mind** within, **Equality** in everything we see, **Proper Understanding** of life and the universe, **Compassion**, helping others in a wise and unconditional way, **See Through** to the truth of impermanence, **Let Go** of all wandering thoughts and attachments, **Freedom** of mind and spirit, **Accord With Conditions**, go along with the environment, **Be Mindful of Ami-**

tabha Buddha, wishing to reach the Pure Land and follow in His Teachings. The first five represent the Buddha's heart, also the virtues of our self-nature. We are presently unable to completely manifest these qualities due to our lack of cultivating the latter five. Diligent practice is needed to bring out these virtues of the Buddha-nature within us.

ဆ The ultimate goal in learning Buddhism is the great Perfection. In all classes of society and fields of occupation, Buddhas and Bodhisattvas act as role models for all people to follow. Students of the Buddha must be good examples for all others, and families which follow the Buddha's teachings must act in a way which is worthy of being the role model for all families. If one is still a student, then one's schoolwork, conduct, and health become an example for one's classmates. This is being a student of the Buddha. In going to work or running a business, one must be a role model for all businessmen to follow. Thus, everything in the Buddhadharma can be number one.

 ‌❧ A family living in perfect wisdom is the most content, fortunate, and happy family in the world.

 ‌❧ Buddhism is the education of wisdom, it encompasses all things, and exceeds the boundaries between countries, races, and religions. Since Buddhism is an education, it is not limited in the boundaries of religion. Followers of all religions are welcome and should learn and cultivate the education of true wisdom.

 ‌❧ In the Sutra of Observing Amitabha and His Pure Land, the 3 Conditions mentioned stands as the basic foundation of cultivation in Buddhism. Upon perfecting the 3 Conditions, one will have complete wisdom, fortune, and virtue.

The first condition consists of four practices based on the fundamental morals of mankind:

1. The practice of filial piety
2. The practice of respecting teachers and elders
3. The practice of harboring compassion and not killing
4. The practice of the 10 Kind Deeds.

The second condition consists of three practices based on cultivating the self:

1. Taking Refuge in the Triple Jewels
2. Understanding the spirit of precepts
3. Being a law-abiding citizen of the world.

The third condition consists of four practices which follow the practices of Bodhisattvas:

1. Giving rise to the Bodhi Mind
2. Deeply believing in the Law of Cause and Effect
3. Studying the teachings of the Large Vehicle
4. Introducing the Teachings to

others.

Altogether, these 11 practices, each having its deep and vast meaning, must be put to use in everyday life, for they are the foundation of the 49 years of teachings spoken by Shakyamuni Buddha.

ଔ Great Vehicle Buddhism in China can be represented by the great Bodhisattvas of the Four Famous Mountains. First is Earth Treasury Bodhisattva of Jiou-Hua Mountain, representing filial piety and respect. Second is Kuan Yin Bodhisattva of Pu-Tuo Mountain, representing compassion. Third is Manjushri Bodhisattva of Wu-Tai Mountain, representing wisdom. Fourth is Universal Worthy Bodhisattva of E-Mei Mountain, representing true practice. These 4 great Bodhisattvas represent the core of cultivation in Buddhism. As beginners, we start learning from Earth Treasury, for the earth is the root of life of all living beings. Because the great earth nurtures all beings and is the treasury of all that is precious, the Buddha uses it to represent our "mind ground" or "mind earth". Our true mind/original nature is complete with infinite wisdom, virtuous abilities, and talents; we must know how to open this treasury in order to attain its benefits. Earth Treasury Bodhisattva teaches us to be filial to our parents and respectful to our teachers, for in these practices lies the key to opening the treasury of our self-nature.

ଔ The field of filial piety is very vast. Our parents have shown us great kindness in bringing us up and educating us, thus, we should not only nurture their aging bodies, but we should also nurture their minds, and let them be happy- this is practicing filial piety.

ଔ Regarding the practice of filial piety, we should strive to do our best in living up to our parents' expectations. When they wish for us to be good persons and benefit the society, we should do so; to act otherwise would be unfilial. For children going to school, it would be unfilial to do poorly at schoolwork, causing one's parents to be worried and disappointed. It would be unfilial if one's conduct was poor, or if one's health was poor, or if one was disrespectful to one's teachers, or if one could not get along with other schoolmates. After reaching adulthood, and entering the society, it would be unfilial to be rebellious towards one's boss, or being unable to cooperate with others at work, causing one's parents at home to worry. From these, we realize how vast the field of cultivating filial piety really is, and that the entire Buddhadharma is actually just teaching the Way of Filial Piety. In Buddhism, the perfection of filial piety is only completed upon reaching the Unsurpassed Understanding (Buddhahood).

ოვ In today's generation, mankind has been seriously polluted in heart, thoughts,

views, spirit, and body, thus leading to
the birth of many strange illnesses. The
root cause of illness and disease is pollution - if one's body and mind are pure,
then one will definitely not fall ill or
grow aged. To not age or become ill is
true happiness and fortune. To attain this
goal, we only need to learn and culti-
vate/practice according to the Buddha's
teachings.

ᘓ In our world today, where foods have
been polluted by toxins and poisons, we
should harbor compassion, for compassion is the antidote for all poisons. A
truly compassionate heart can neutralize
all poisons. The Buddha once said, "All
dharmas arise from the mind." Thus, a
pure, equanimous, and understanding
mind/heart naturally brings health to
one's body.

ᘓ When we recite morning and evening
ceremonies in front of the Buddha and
Bodhisattva images, it is just as if we

were vowing to abide by their teachings right in their presence. Morning recitation acts as a reminder, preventing us from forgetting the Buddha's teachings, and reminding us to act accordingly in the course of the day. Evening recitation is a reflection of today's practice, checking to see if we acted accordingly to the Buddha's teachings. If we did, then we should work even harder next time, if not, then we must reform, seeking to renew ourselves with each day. Only practicing in this way can true benefits be attained. Morning and evening recitations are the most basic practices in learning Buddhism. It is necessary to remind ourselves each day, and reflect and reform.

ꭾ One who wishes to become a student of the Buddha should first learn from Maitreya Buddha, or better known in America as "Happy Buddha". Maitreya Buddha represents the most basic conditions necessary to become Buddhist - a smiling face and a big heart. (Represented by his big belly). We must recognize that all Buddha images serve to remind us of the Teachings, and are not idols or gods of worship. "Happy Buddha" teaches us to give rise to an equanimous mind, and be happy; thus being able to enter the Buddha Way.

ରଘ The content of the Buddha's teachings is infinitely deep and vast, one is unable to speak of it all, for the flavor of it is unfathomable. Understanding it can bring great help to our living, work, and dealing with all people, matters, and affairs. Buddhism truly surpasses the boundaries of nationality, races, and religions - there isn't a single thing it cannot encompass. The Buddha's teachings is truly a very complete education.

TAKING REFUGE IN THE TRIPLE JEWELS

❧

Taking Refuge means to return and rely. When we take refuge in the Buddha, we are returning from our deluded state of mind and relying upon an Awakened, Understanding mind. When we take refuge in the Dharma, we are returning from deviant views and relying upon proper views and understanding. When we take refuge in the Sangha, we are returning from pollution and disharmony and relying upon Purity of Mind and the Six Principles of Living in Harmony. Taking refuge in the Triple Jewels restores the complete wisdom and abilities of our Self-Nature. We will attain Purity, Equality, Honesty, Freedom, Compassion, and overall, True Happiness.

THE BUDDHA JEWEL

"Buddha" is a Sanskrit word which means 'Awareness and Understanding'. When we take refuge in the Buddha, we vow to return from blind faith and delusion and rely upon

Understanding and Awareness as a way of life. Images of the Buddha serve as a reminder for us to practice awareness and understanding, and are not objects of worship. Bowing and showing respect towards these images are only ways to counter arrogance and cultivate humility. This is taking refuge in the Buddha.

THE DHARMA JEWEL

"Dharma" means 'Right Understanding and Views.' Delusion has obstructed us from seeing the true face of people and the reality behind matters and objects. This has caused us to look at life and the universe in a distorted and deviant way. When delusion is cleared and our minds are pure to an extent, we give rise to wisdom. With wisdom, we are able to see all people and matters completely and clearly. When our hearts are pure, we can see the past, present, and future. Only when we have clearly seen the Whole can our viewpoint and Understanding be considered 'Right'.

The Buddha's mind is pure without the slightest pollution and therefore sees everything clearly and entirely. We can rely upon the Sutras (recorded teachings of the Buddha) because they speak entirely of the truths the Buddha has seen. They teach and show us the way to attain Purity of Mind, to see life and universe most clearly, and become just like the Buddhas. When we encounter Sutras, we should immediately bring forth a mind of respect and remind ourselves to cultivate Right Understanding and Views. This is taking refuge in the Dharma.

THE SANGHA JEWEL

"Sangha" means 'purity and harmony'. Today's world is full of pollution. Pollution of mind, spirit, views, and body. Even the earth and the atmosphere are hazardly polluted. The Buddha taught, "The environment changes according to the mind." We should return from all these pollutions and rely upon purity of mind. Purity of Mind is the key to saving our Earth.

There is also great disharmony in our world today, among spouses, families, friends, societies, and countries which has brought us much suffering and disasters. The Buddha taught us to rely upon the Six Principles of Living in Harmony to establish harmonious relationships between ourselves and others.

"Sangha" also refers to a group of four or more persons who practice the Buddha's teachings and abides by the Six Principle of Living in Harmony. This includes the left-home people we may encounter at various places. When we see left-home people, we should immediately give rise to a mind of purity and harmony. This is taking refuge in the Sangha.

THE THREE REFUGES

*To the Buddha I return and rely,
returning from delusions and
relying upon Awareness and Understanding.*

*To the Dharma I return and rely,
returning from erroneous views and
relying upon Proper Views and Understanding.*

*To the Sangha I return and rely,
returning from pollutions and disharmony
and relying upon Purity of Mind and the
Six Principles of Living in Harmony.*

How Housewives Can Cultivate the Bodhisattva Way in Everyday Life

It must be very tiresome to do the same kind of work everyday, and especially for housewives. It seems as if one cannot be free from household chores for a single day, and many are greatly troubled by their duties. But if we can learn to change our way of looking at things, we will be able to perform our chores with great joy.

The problem lies in that worldly people are very much attached to the "self". They think, "*I'm* doing all this work; Poor *me*, *I'm* so tired; Why should *I* do this for them?...". The more they think this way, the more afflicted they become. If we were to learn the Bodhisattva Way (the Way of Understanding/Enlightenment) and vow to universally help all living beings, then our viewpoint would be much different.

In following the Bodhisattva Path, the first thing we should learn is the Practice of Giving. By serving her family at home, the housewife Bodhisattva is already cultivating Giving. Giving includes the Giving of Wealth, the Giving of Teaching, and the Giving of Fearlessness. The Giving of Wealth can be divided into outer wealth and inner wealth. For example, outer wealth refers to making money for your family and providing the means for living. Inner wealth refers to using your physical energy and wisdom to support your family. So, the practice of giving can be completed perfectly at home.

When we do our housework with care and organize our home to be clean and neat, this is bringing comfort to the family and admiration from our neighbors; this is cultivating the Practice of Abiding by Precepts. Abiding by precepts simply means abiding by rules - rules of the country, society, and family, and doing everything in an organized and proper way. In having endurance doing our chores without complaining or feeling fatigue, this is cultivating the Practice of Patience. In seeking improvement everyday, hoping that tomorrow's attainment will exceed that of today's, this is cultivating the Practice of Diligence. In performing one's various duties daily but still maintaining a pure and undeluded heart, this is cultivating the Practice of Concentration in Purity of Mind, being apart from discriminations and attachments. From within purity of mind, one will give rise to wisdom, and will be filled with inner peace and happiness, this is cultivating the Practice of Wisdom. Thus, with true understanding, we will discover that these Six Principles Cultivated by Bodhisattvas (Giving, Abiding by Precepts, Patience, Diligence, Concentration in Purity of Mind, and Wisdom) can be practiced to perfection in the everyday acts of dusting, sweeping, washing, and cooking.

Once we have performed our duties well, we become role models for housewives all over the world, and an example for all families to follow. Thus, not only can we help our neighbors, but extended, we can influence society, the country, and even the world in a positive way. From this we come to see that in dusting, sweeping, washing, and cooking, a housewife bodhisattva is actually carrying out the great vow of helping all living beings. This is truly being a student of the Buddha. So, if we can contemplate our duties as described above, we will be overflowed with peace and happiness in our work. How could anything trouble us then?

We must remember that the most important factor in learning and cultivating the Buddha's teachings is that one must be able to practice them in everyday life. If not, then studying the Buddha's teachings would be meaningless. Understanding this, we would be able to practice the Six Principles Cultivated by Bodhisattvas at our work and office. A Bodhisattva, in all classes of society and fields of occupation, whether appearing as a man, woman, elder, or child, cultivates by keeping to his/her rightful place in the country, society, and family, and living up to his/her own responsibilities. Cultivation and living are one - this is the lifestyle of enlightened beings.

LIVING BUDDHISM
SELECTED PASSAGES

  Buddhism is an education, not a religion. We do not worship the Buddha, we respect him as a teacher. His teachings enable us to leave suffering and attain true happiness.

  We should treat all people with respect and sincerity. We must be responsible for our actions and careful when handling others' properties. Be conservative with speech and actions to avoid harming others.

  We should show our gratitude to those who have shown us kindness, such as parents, teachers, and even the society. Everyone in the society is interdependent and inter-related, we should practice good deeds to repay them.

  How many people recognize the kindness shown by parents? Usually, people do not realize until they themselves become parents or lose their parents. We should show our gratitude through practicing filial piety by being responsible, considerate, and obedient to our parents.

𝕫 To be a poor, content, and happy person is better than being one who is rich, worried, and afflicted with greed.

𝕫 Buddhism is a teaching which shows us how to live a happy, fulfilling, and content life.

𝕫 True Love is undiscriminating, unattaching, and unconditional, we should share this love with all beings. This is called compassion.

𝕫 If we wish to bring peace to the world, we must start by changing our evil ways. World peace stems from inner peace.

𝕫 Our goal in studying the Buddha's teachings and cultivation is to attain complete understanding of life and the universe.

𝒜 Be considerate and kind in your speech. To put-down another person is only proving your own arrogance and lack of self confidence to others.

𝒜 Life is short and fragile, why not cultivate kindness instead of committing acts which cause harm to living beings?

𝒜 Practicing virtue is to keep a kind heart, speak kind words, and do kind acts to benefit others.

𝒜 Wise persons do not harbor feelings of gain or loss. In this way, they constantly dwell in the joy of possessing great peace of mind.

𝒜 The point of practicing giving and charity is to forsake greed, hatred, ignorance, and arrogance.

֍ When helping others, we should think about benefiting the entire society or even the world instead of limiting our help to just the ones we love. Expanding the boundaries of our care for others makes our lives more meaningful, full of freedom and happiness.

֍ The Buddha's teachings are a teaching of wisdom. Living Buddhism is to fill our lives with utmost wisdom and happiness.

֍ In all circumstances, we must first reflect upon ourselves. Confucius once said, "Do not give to others what you yourself do not desire". This is teaching us to keep a humane and sincere heart. If we want others to smile at us, we must first smile at others. In dealing with affairs, we must not seek personal gain but should work for the public welfare.

֍ A true cultivator does not see the faults of others. When we think of others' faults, it becomes our own affliction. Everyone has their good and bad sides, but we must learn to look at the good points of others and strive to respect all beings.

THE ART
OF
LIVING II

Given by Venerable Master Chin Kung

"The Art of Living II"
By Venerable Master Chin Kung
Dallas, Texas
July 1995

Buddhism instructs us how to live happy and fulfilling lives. It was transmitted to China in 67 AD and since then, has spread and flourished throughout the country. However, anything that has been passed down for a long period can be expected to experience some distortion and Buddhism is no exception.

Originally, Buddhism was Buddha Shakyamuni's teaching of perfection of enlightenment for all sentient beings in the nine realms. Unfortunately, over the last two to three hundred years, some began to regard it as a religion. Then, in the past twenty to thirty years it began to be viewed as a philosophy.

However, the most disastrous of all is its distortion by some into a cult. These have seriously misled people away from the original teachings. If we commit ourselves to the practice, we need to clearly understand exactly what the Buddha taught us.

A few years ago in San Francisco, I gave a talk titled "To Understand Buddhism." Unfortunately, due to the one and a half-hour time constraint, I was unable to elaborate as much as I had wanted to. Then, several months later, Mr. David Zheng invited me to Miami. He both hosted and provided the English translation for my seven-day lecture series on Buddhism titled "To Understand Buddhism". The talks were video taped at that time and later published. To understand the Buddha's teachings is our first and most basic lesson. Practicing Buddhism and not knowing what the goals are can reduce our practice to blind superstition.

First, the Buddha is our teacher and not a god. Bodhisattvas are our senior classmates with whom we share equal status. Buddhism is an education. What does it teach? The Buddha's forty-nine years of teaching are recorded as sutras. These have been combined with sutra commentaries by great masters throughout history into a dense collection called The Buddhist Canon, of which there are over thirty versions in existence. These teachings explain the truth about life and the universe. Life refers to us and the universe refers to our living environment and beyond. What is more relevant than to understand the relationship between the universe and us?

Several years ago, I was lecturing

to professors at the Universities of Beijing, Nanjing and Liouling. Upon learning that Buddhism is an education, my audience was astonished. Then, two years ago I learned that there were one hundred seventy professors across China studying the teachings. This is a good sign. We ought to first change our perceptions and understand the nature of this unsurpassed education, to fully benefit from it.

The Buddha told us that an enlightened person is one who completely understands about life and the universe. A Buddha is a being who is perfectly enlightened while a Bodhisattva, according to Master Xuan Tsuang, is an "awakened, sentient being." The element that differentiates us from Buddhas and Bodhisattvas is the state of consciousness or enlightenment. Enlightened beings are free and independent in any environment while we are not. The Chinese have a saying "When one is constricted by society, one is unable to act according to one's will." For instance, almost everyone wishes to make a fortune in this lifetime, but look around, how many people's dreams have actually come true? Buddhist sutras have provided us with methods to achieve whatever we wish; to stay healthy, young and happy as well as to end the cycle of birth and death. Praying to the Buddhas, Bodhisattvas or spirits simply does not do it.

The sutras have taught us the way to take control of our destiny. If we follow the teachings, we can have what we wish for. However, if we fail to achieve our goal, it is because we either have applied the wrong method or misinterpreted the meanings within the sutras. Buddhism is a teaching of wisdom as only wisdom can resolve our problems and fulfill our wishes.

How do we gain wisdom? Many people who grew up in our modern society would agree that wisdom is gained from information or knowledge. The Buddha told us the opposite! He taught us that wisdom is already within our self-nature; it does not come from the outside. Upon reaching enlightenment, the Sixth Patriarch of Zen, Master Hui-Neng reported to his teacher that wisdom is something we all possess and that it is innate. Our good fortune, capability and wisdom are complete; none of them can be obtained externally. The Buddha teaches us to look for them within our mind, our pure mind. Therefore, Buddhism is a study of the inner self.

Earlier this year, a group of professors, most of them from the University of

Taiwan and the Central Educational Research Center, requested me to talk on the <u>Diamond Sutra</u>. Although I had not lectured on this sutra for almost twenty years, I gladly accepted the invitation as an opportunity to leave future Buddhists a lecture series to aid them in their studies.

The <u>Diamond Sutra</u> is truly an important part of Mahayana practice as well as the core of Zen practice. It concentrates on the understanding of wisdom. Due to the advocation of Zen's Fifth and Sixth Patriarchs, this sutra became widely known in China. Over five thousand eight hundred words in length, it is too profound for most people to completely understand. There have been several hundred explanations or commentaries written on this sutra alone throughout Chinese history. Earlier in this century, Mr. Wei-Nong

Jiang, who spent forty years studying this sutra, wrote what has become a well-read commentary. He combined the essence of both the ancient and current commentaries to make it easier for people to understand the sutra and thus, the true meanings of life and the universe.

The <u>Diamond Sutra</u>, like other sutras, contains the principles and methods to achieve enlightenment. If we can master the principle and cultivate with confidence, we will become enlightened regardless of the method we choose. However, if we are not achieving improvement in our daily practice, then we must have overlooked the principles and methods of the sutra.

For many years, I have been lecturing on the Pure Land method. Someone asked me, "Teacher, you have been speaking of the Pure Land teachings for so long, why are you now lecturing on the <u>Diamond Sutra</u>?" When you think about it, the <u>Diamond Sutra</u>, the <u>Amitabha Sutra</u> and the <u>Infinite Life Sutra</u> are all the same in that they encourage us to recite the Buddha's name, without any attachment, in order to be born into the Western Pure Land. If we did not already have a high degree of wisdom, good roots, merits and good conditions, we would not have chosen the Pure Land School as our practice.

When I was young, I made the mistake of thinking that this school was not a high level practice. Fortunately, I met good teachers who tried to convince me of its importance. Still I was unable to completely accept it. The confidence I now possess comes from having lectured on the <u>Avatamsaka</u>

(Flower Adornment) Sutra for seventeen years. It tells of how Manjusri Bodhisattva, Samantabhadra (Universal Worthy) Bodhisattva, Maitreya Bodhisattva, the forty-one levels of enlightened Bodhisattvas, Sudhana and the fifty-three spiritual guides all turned to the Pure Land School in the end. As I became convinced of its importance, I started to study the Pure Land sutras. I realized that practicing the Pure Land method was actually the highest level of Buddha Shakyamuni's teachings and of all the Buddhas in the ten directions as they strove to help all sentient beings achieve enlightenment.

I have lectured on the Diamond Sutra, the Infinite Life and the Visualization sutras. They all are concerned with the right and proper way of living. The Diamond Sutra speaks of the principle while the Infinite Life Sutra and the

<u>Visualization Sutra</u> speak of the specifics in practice and attainment. Mr. Wei-Nong Jiang emphasized that one who cultivates prajna, innate wisdom, should chant the name of Buddha Amitabha in order to be born into the Pure Land. Practitioners need to completely understand the Buddha's teachings because they lead us to perfect, free-spirited and prosperous living. If we misinterpret the teachings, then we will not benefit from them. While Buddhism emphasizes the principles, it puts more stress on our practice. If our practice fails to follow these principles then we have missed the point.

Take the <u>Diamond Sutra</u> for example. As it begins, the Buddha takes us into his daily life. This is unlike other Mahayana sutras in which he would release radiant light at the beginning of his talk. However, this talk is all about everyday life! Every action the Buddha has taken has revealed his virtues and merits due to his commitment of practicing Buddhahood through infinite lifetimes.

The <u>Avatamsaka (Flower Adornment) Sutra</u> tells us that "One is all and all is one." One refers to a matter or subject, for example, dressing is one activity, eating is another. From the moment we decide to begin our practice till the time we achieve Enlightenment, our merits are accumulated and revealed through our efforts and commitment. Daily activities are the way of practice; however, most of us cannot see this. Why not? Because of our lack of wisdom. Subhuti, one of the Buddha's main students, explained it for us. We all get up every morning, dress and eat. What do we have to show for this? Infinite lifetimes of committing misdeeds and the resultant sufferings due to incorrect understanding of the purpose of life and our environment.

Buddhas and Bodhisattvas show us the art and the correct way of living. If we understand the Diamond Sutra, we will understand everything around us and in the universe. Beings who do understand are called Buddhas and Bodhisattvas: those who do not are called ordinary people. We all possess the capabilities of Buddhas, but we are temporarily lost and have forgotten what we possess. This is why we must practice to learn how to live our lives. Practicing Buddhism means correcting our erroneous thoughts and actions in our daily lives. Those of us who understand focus on the root of the problem, which means we focus on correcting our thoughts while others focus on their actions. By only correcting our actions, we may gain some improvement; however, this is similar to only taking care of the branches and leaves of a tree while neglecting its roots. The most effective way, as pointed out in the <u>Diamond Sutra</u>, is to correct our thoughts by attacking the roots of all that is wrong or erroneous.

What are the guidelines for practicing Buddhism? Buddha Shakyamuni told us they are The Three Learnings, which are precepts (rules), concentration and wisdom. Precepts refer to following all of the Buddha's teachings, not just the basic five or ten precepts. They also include following customs, rules and laws wherever we are. Law-abiding people have a clear conscience, so their minds are peaceful and they can more easily concentrate, whereas, people who often break the law are generally unable to concentrate. Therefore, following rules and obeying laws enables us to achieve the concentration that allows us to uncover the wisdom that we already possess.

The <u>Platform Sutra</u> of the Sixth Patriarch Hui-Neng is praiseworthy for its high level of wisdom. We can understand why the Sixth Patriarch told his master that he often generated wisdom. We, on the other hand, often generate affliction. He achieved this high level because his mind was pure. Our minds are filled with afflictions, attachments, discriminating and wandering thoughts: all causes of reincarnation. To alter this course requires us to cleanse our minds of these pollutants. To accomplish this, Buddha Shakyamuni gave us the forementioned three guidelines which are also contained in the <u>Infinite Life Sutra</u>, the full title of which is <u>The Buddha Speaks of the Infinite Life Sutra of Adornment, Purity, Equality and Enlightenment of the Mahayana School</u>. Purity refers to precepts; equality refers to deep concentration; enlightenment refers to wisdom. These are also expressed as the Triple Jewels, representing respectively the Sangha, the Dharma and the Buddha. Please do not mistake the physical images of the Triple Jewels for their true essence. The <u>Diamond Sutra</u> clearly tells us "One who sees images of oneself, other human beings, all beings and life is not a Bodhisattva." In other words, looking beyond physical aspects is the correct way to understand these guidelines.

The Buddha represents enlightenment. The Dharma, symbolized by sutras, represents the Buddha's wisdom, virtue and proper understanding of life and the universe. The Sangha represents purity of the six senses, having no pollution. The Three Jewels are being enlightened and not deluded, proper and not deviated, pure and not polluted. When we take refuge in the Triple Jewels, we request guidance from a Monk or Nun regarding purity, equality and enlightenment. It is important to understand this at the beginning of our practice. We need to use an awakened mind to perform in our daily lives. The Dharma comes from the self-nature within. The goal of the learning process is to find our true self and to let go of our incorrect state of mind.

This incorrect state of mind is embroiled in a non-stop rush of thoughts. When we let go of all our wandering and discriminating thoughts, our true self will surface and so then will true wisdom. Only through the process of concentration and purification can wisdom flourish. To accomplish this, the Pure Land School uses the Buddha Name Chanting Method, while Zen uses a different method. Every practice has its own method to accomplish the same goal of enlightenment. All ways of practice are equal.

Buddha Shakyamuni taught us innumerable ways of practice. It is up to us to choose the one that is compatible with the depth of our root nature, level of achievement and manner of living. Regardless of the practice we choose, the three basic guidelines are enlightenment, right and proper thoughts, and purity.

We have to be extremely careful living in our time. The <u>Surangama Sutra</u> tells us that we are now living in the

Dharma-ending age when pollution of both the mind and the environment are at their worst. There are countless numbers of deviated thinking teachers in this time who are creating great chaos. It is crucial that we use the standards taught by the Buddha to distinguish between proper and deviated.

The Pure Land sutras teach us how to start our practice with the Three Conditions. These three have been the foundation of Buddhahood throughout eternity. All Buddhas say that Buddhahood is achieved through any one of an infinite number of methods. However, every method requires the Three Conditions as a foundation. This is similar to building a house. No matter how many houses we are building, each requires a good foundation. The First Condition includes:

(A) Showing respect and care for ones parents,

(B) Listening carefully to and respecting teachers and elders,

(C) Showing compassion by not killing and

(D) Following the Ten Good Conducts.

If we act accordingly, then we will benefit from this First Condition.

The practice of Filial Piety is showing respect and caring for one's parents. The foundation of Chinese civilization has been built on filial piety, as was Buddhism in India. The Chinese character "Shiao" means filial piety. The top part means old age while the bottom part means son. When the two are put together, it gives us the meaning of one entity. It is vastly expansive and never-ending. It speaks of the generations before ours and of those to follow.

I have met many westerners who asked me about the Chinese tradition of paying respect to ancestors they did not even know about. They did not understand that all of life is just one entity with no beginning and no end. Only Buddhism can carry filial piety to perfection.

Being filial does not simply mean taking care of parents financially, it goes beyond that to helping them cultivate their minds to a higher level of living and wisdom. Buddha Shakyamuni, our "Original Teacher", taught this to us. If our actions such as not doing well at school, not following rules and listening to teachers, not getting along with friends, relatives or co-workers; generally not living up to our parent's expectations worry them, then we have done poorly at filial piety. In other words, making our parents happy is part of filial piety. But most importantly, not until we reach the state of Buddhahood, will we perfectly fulfill filial respect for our parents and ancestors.

The second part of the First Condition is following and respecting teachers and elders. In his forty-nine years of teaching, Buddha Shakyamuni showed us how to correctly live our lives. Following his teachings shows our respect for him.

The third part of the First Condition is cultivating compassion and not killing. There is a big difference between love and compassion. Love comes from feelings; compassion comes from wisdom. Love is unstable and unreliable. We may love someone today but not tomorrow. When someone tells us that he or she loves or hates us, we would do well not to take it too seriously. However, compassion is for forever because it is based on the wisdom that is part of the true mind, our original self. It is not based on emotion. We can start by showing compassion and kindness for our family and keep expanding until we include every sentient being in the ten directions. Developing this level of compassion is another part of the cultivation that will lead us to enlightenment.

The fourth part of the first Condition includes following the Ten Good Conducts. These are no killing, stealing, sexual misconduct, lying, abusive language, bearing tales, seductive words, greed, anger or ignorance. The first three are disciplines of the body, the next four are disciplines of the mouth and the last three are disciplines of the mind.

One who follows the Ten Good Conducts in their daily life acquires a solid foundation for self-cultivation. To be truthful, understanding the principles is easy; however, putting them into practice requires a high level of wisdom. There is some flexibility in practicing the Ten Good Conducts, which is why the guidance of a good teacher and the encouragement of our fellow classmates or practitioners are essential in helping us to attain enlightenment in this lifetime. This is why the respect and sincerity towards our teachers and elders are part of the foundation and a prerequisite for our cultivation.

Having achieved the First Condition in this area will have a positive effect on one's prosperity and well being in both the human and the heavenly worlds. The sutras call those who accomplish this, "good men and good women" because they are ready to accept the teachings and follow the precepts to attain purity of mind.

The Second Condition is:

(A) Abiding by taking refuge in the Three Jewels of the Buddha, Dharma and Sangha,

(B) Following the precepts, laws and customs and

(C) Behaving in a dignified and proper manner.

I have discussed these earlier in this talk.

The Third Condition is:

(A) Generating the Bodhi mind,

(B) Deeply believing in the Law of Cause and Effect

(C) Reciting and upholding Mahayana sutras and

(D) Encouraging others to advance on the path to enlightenment.

In generating the Bodhi mind, one commits oneself to achieving ultimate enlightenment. Enlightenment refers to a perfect and complete understanding of life and the universe. If we cannot reach it then we can at least obtain a clear understanding of it.

The second part of the Third Condition is deeply believing in the Law of Cause and Effect. **Nothing is beyond this law.** All other laws in the universe revolve around it. However, one can control one's own cause and effect. How can this be done? There is nothing we can do about past causes once the thought or action has been done, but we can control the "condition." For a cause to generate an effect, a condition has to exist. By controlling the circumstance or condition, one prevents the cause from coming into effect. For example, if we place a seed on a rock, it will not grow. However, if we plant it in fertile soil where the sun shines and water it carefully, then it can grow. Once we learn how to control the condition, then everything we wish for can be obtained. Knowing this and acting accordingly, we will be liberated from aging, sickness and the cycle of birth and death.

All dharmas are generated by the mind. For example, why does a person become old? When a person reaches a certain age, he or she starts thinking "old." I have spoken with a number of Buddhist doctors about why people become old. They agreed with me that when people are working, they do not think about old age. However, after they have been retired a few years they look as if they were twenty years older! Why? Retired people who are no longer working start thinking every day about becoming old. After a while, they start to age more rapidly and then to become sick. Once they get sick, they start thinking about going to the hospital. All this came about from wandering thoughts.

However, this is not the case for people who successfully practice the Buddha Name Chanting Method. My late teacher, Mr. Bing-Nan Lee, lived to be ninety-seven years old but looked more like seventy. He cooked for himself and washed his own clothes. Not until his last two years did he accept any care. He was healthy, had a strong voice and was giving lectures up until two weeks before he passed away. Why? He did not think about sickness or old age. We will not get sick if we do not think about getting sick, we will not age if we do not think about old age and we will not die if we do not think about death.

Buddhism provides the principles, methods and practices to accomplish this. The art of living can be mastered once we fully understand and practice Buddhism. It teaches us to maintain a healthy mind. A healthy mind creates a healthy body. All sickness comes from pollution and the worst pollution is that of the mind. The Buddha called this pollution the Three Poisons of Greed, Anger and Ignorance. Between the pollution of the environment and that of our mind how can we not get sick? However, even with the worst pollution around us, a person who is free of the three poisons will not become sick.

All the Buddhas and Bodhisattvas set examples so beings can see that we may live happy, prosperous and perfect lives. Seeing this, people will want to follow our example. We are supposed to be role models for society. However, if people see Buddhists living a miserable life, no one will want to learn from us!

The more we understand the Buddha's teachings, the more joy we will receive from them. To comprehend the profound meaning within, one needs to practice earnestly. Understanding and cultivation are equally important in complementing each other to attain even deeper understanding and cultivation. Achieving this, one will experience true inner joy and peace. If we are not experiencing some of this joy and are instead filled with worries then we need to take a good look at ourselves, to see whether or not we are practicing in accordance with the teachings. If not, find out where the problem lies and correct it. Doing this properly, we will be on the right path of Buddhism.

Regardless of the situations we encounter, adverse or favorable, keep focused and concentrate on achieving enlightenment. The fifty-three visits that Sudhana had in the <u>Flower Adornment Sutra</u> represented people from all walks of life portrayed by fifty-three enlightened Bodhisattvas. This shows us that people of any profession can become a Buddha or Bodhisattva. We do not have to change our job or the environment, in which we live but can practice wherever we are. The benefits begin the minute we start to correct our thoughts and actions.

We would do well to live our lives

with a clear mind and to be proper in thought and action, not being tempted by erroneous influences. If we are able to do this, then no matter which method we choose we will be true followers of the Buddha. As our daily thinking becomes clearer, our mind will become purer, enabling us to live happier, peaceful and fulfilling lives.

When I heard of a suggestion made by the late Mr. Lian-Jui Xia to use the name Pure Land Buddhist Learning Center instead of the traditional name of temple, I thought it was appropriate for today's society. Buddhism has always been forward thinking not backward. It has adapted to existing cultures and localities. When Buddhism first came to China, it took on aspects of the Chinese culture. The temples had a Chinese appearance, the monks and nuns clothing was in the Chinese style. If the temples had followed Indian design, the Chinese would not have wanted to enter such a foreign looking place. The teachings were interpreted in a way that enabled the Chinese people to merge them into their daily lives, thus they were readily accepted. The <u>Diamond Sutra</u> tells us that nothing is permanent, while the <u>Surangama Sutra</u> explains that everything should accord with the minds of sentient beings. All this is to remind us to accord with local conditions.

At a talk one time in Miami, there were quite a few Buddhists who were westerners. I told them that Buddhism had not yet officially come to America. They asked why I had said that when Buddhism was very popular in America. I asked them," Have you ever seen

Buddhist statues with features that resemble a westerner?" They briefly thought about it and realized that what I had said was true. When Buddhism spread to China, pictures and statues of Buddhas and Bodhisattvas adopted Chinese features. In Japan, they have Japanese features. The same applies to Thailand, Tibet and so on. Buddhas and Bodhisattvas do not have only one fixed appearance, rather they appear in the form that is most acceptable and comfortable for the local people.

Furthermore, Buddhism adapts to take on the aspects of the local culture. In America, a typical Buddhist temple needs to look like the White House and not like a traditional Chinese temple. When Americans see a Chinese temple, they would think of it as foreign and might not feel comfortable going in. However, if the buildings look like the White House, they would go in uninvited! Do you not think that they would be happy to see Buddhas and Bodhisattvas with western features? They certainly would.

We need to remember that Buddhism is an education. As it spreads through America, it will take on a more western appearance just as it did when Indian teachers brought it to China, where it took on a Chinese appearance. As Buddhism adapts to new cultures, it will remain current with the times, thus appealing to more people. Those, who accept it, will be able to apply the teachings in solving their personal as well as social problems. As Buddhism is accepted, it will bring peace and prosperity to those people as well as to the whole world. Understanding this will help us to begin our cultivation.

After the Pure Land Learning Center was officially established, Five Guidelines were set up for practice:

1) The Three Conditions,
2) The Six Principles of Harmony,
3) The Three Learnings,
4) The Six Paramitas or Principles and
5) The Ten Great Vows of Universal Worthy Bodhisattva.

These Five Guidelines can bring us happiness and prosperity if we make them a part of our daily lives.

The Six Paramitas or Principles, one of these Five Guidelines, represent the six goals that Bodhisattvas practice. They are giving, precepts, patience, diligence, deep concentration and wisdom. A homemaker, who daily performs the same chores and constantly complains about them, will find that with this attitude, he or she has created a certain destiny within the cycle of birth and death. On the other hand, if one is awakened and devotes himself or herself to accomplishing the Six Principles, the results will be quite different.

For example, the Principle of Giving is achieved when one takes care of the family with wisdom and tireless labor. The Principle of Precepts is achieved when one sets priorities and puts things into order; the Principle of Patience when one increases patience while working; the Principle of Diligence when one tries to improve daily; the Principle of Concentration when one is no longer affected by external factors and the Principle of Wisdom when one is clear-minded. A pure mind has no attachments therefore it never gets tired. On the other hand, a polluted mind becomes easily tired without having doing much. The difference lies in the way we think, when this changes, so will the results. Wherever one is, at work or with friends, one can strive to achieve the Six Principles. Cultivation is not being separated from family or society, but is perfected within one's daily life. One, who truly knows how to cultivate, accumulates infinite good fortune and merits.

In conclusion, the most important principles of the Buddha's teachings are having purity of mind, thoroughly seeing through to true reality, letting go of all worries and attachments and serving all sentient beings with a joyful heart.

May you all learn and practice the "Art of Living" so that your life will be happy and fulfilling.

Questions and Answers

Question. How do we purify our minds so we can remain forever young?

Answer. This is a good question. The sutras tell us that anything that has a physical image is unreal. We can apply these physical images, but we cannot foster attachments for them. Attachments create impurity in our mind, deterring us from achieving enlightenment. This applies to all forms of practice in Buddhism. Even the Pure Land School, which many agree is the easiest to practice, requires that although one who wishes to be born into the Pure Land can take their remaining karma with them, they cannot have any existing worries or attachments. Therefore, a person with worries or attachments cannot transcend the cycle of birth and death. Life becomes harder as we pass through the cycles of rebirth.

Earlier in this talk, I spoke of filial piety. Up until 1995, the only attachment I had left was for my ninety-one year old mother, who lived in China. When I met with her about ten years earlier in Hong Kong, I persuaded her to practice the Buddha Name Chanting Method. When I spoke with her on the telephone several years ago, she still had strong attachments for her sons and grandchildren. Not until a year ago did she finally let go of all attachments. She told me that she had seen Buddha Amitabha twice and Guan Yin Bodhisattva once. In addition, she had prior knowledge of when she would be leaving this world. On May 29, 1995, she passed on and was born into the Western Pure Land. At her funeral, people were aware of a radiant glow and a pleasing yet unfamiliar fragrance. Her complexion appeared similar to that of a live person. After eight days, her body was still soft. Upon her cremation, more than three hundred sharira, or relics, were found. All this is evidence that she had been successfully born into the Pure Land.

In conclusion, once we are rid of worries and attachments we can go to the Western Pure Land whenever we wish. By maintaining a pure, non-discriminating, compassionate and kind heart, one holds the key to remaining youthful.

Question. Why do some Buddhists exclude the five pungent vegetables from their diet?

Answer. Some Buddhists who follow a strict diet do not eat the five pungent vegetables; onions, garlic, chives, green onions and leeks. The Buddha said that these adversely affect those who are in the early stages of cultivation. If eaten cooked, they produce hormones. Eaten raw, they may affect the liver, leading one to become irritable and less able to concentrate. Please understand that this only happens if you eat them in large quantities. There is no problem if a moderate amount is used for cooking.

The same applies for alcohol and intoxicants. Intoxication can be a factor in causing erroneous behavior. The Buddha warned people against alcohol or intoxicants to guide them in the avoidance of committing misdeeds due to intoxication. Therefore, the precepts that the Buddha set forth really depend upon the environment and the situation that we are in.

Our society is different from that of Buddha Shakyamuni's. If he were to re appear in this world, I am sure the Buddha would encourage the use of garlic simply because it can be used to cure some diseases, especially lung disease.

Many years ago, I was teaching at the Eastern Buddhist College. During that period, we found out that a few of the students had lung diseases. Dr. Tang, who was one of the professors, suggested that they use garlic for treatment. He told us of an event that had happened in China some time ago. A patient was told by his doctor that due to his end stage of TB, he only had three months to live. The patient's family was also told to let him have anything he asked for, with one condition; that he lived apart from his family. His family therefore, built a room for him to live in o vegetable garden and delivered meals to him every day.

In that garden, grew a large amount of garlic. Due to his isolation and boredom, he tried the garlic raw and discovered that he enjoyed the taste of it. Soon the garlic became more of a snack for him. Three months later, he was still alive, and months after that, he was becoming healthier and healthier. His family found it strange and thinking there had been a misdiagnosis took him back to the hospital.

The doctor was astonished at what he saw and immediately gathered a group of specialists to investigate his patient's case. Finally, they found out it was the garlic that cured the disease! From then on, many medicines for lung disease have been made with garlic. Regretfully, when Dr. Tang suggested that those students use garlic for treatment, his suggestion was not accepted. The students did not want to violate the precepts even though their illness was contagious. Therefore, precepts have to be flexible and to consider environment conditions. Nowadays, almost everything we eat, such as, meat, fish and even vegetables, contains either chemicals or preservatives, which are harmful to us. In addition, we are seeing more and more people with diseases that have not previously existed.

Even the taste of meat is different now. Years ago, chicks and piglets were raised in the open, so they were happier and that affected the taste of the meat. Now animals are raised in a narrow space with no place to move. Do you think they are happy? I heard that in Taiwan, the piglets are injected with chemicals so they grow more quickly. Their life span is only six months and the chickens only live for six weeks! Even vegetables and grains are no exceptions to being contaminated. How could we not get sick?

Therefore, garlic is good for us, although it is harmful to our eyes when taken in large quantities.

Question. The Buddha taught us not to kill, but what should we do about insects such as mosquitoes and flies?

Answer. The Buddha not only taught us to protect all animals, but also plants. Even plants have lives and grow with dignity. Therefore, unless there is absolutely no space for us to walk around them, we should not step on them because that behavior is an insult and disrespectful to the plants.

Normally, when a tree is as tall as human, there is a tree spirit. In ancient times, monks often lived in mountain huts. Three days before they cut a tree to build the hut, they would respectfully tell of their intention and ask the tree spirit to move to a safe place. This method can be applied to insects. In order to keep our houses and environment clean and our family healthy, we can stand in front of a statue of the Buddha or Bodhisattva three days before our actions and ask the insects to move. Some people who have done so with sincere and kind hearts have received good results.

The Ten Recitation Method

The Ten-Recitation method is a simple, convenient, effective way to practice Buddha Name Recitation. It is especially suitable for those who find little time in the day for cultivation. Practicing this method helps us to regain mindfulness of Buddha Amitabha and brings us peace and clarity in the present moment.

The practice begins first thing in the morning when we wake up. We sit up straight and clearly recite Buddha Amitabha's name ten times with an undisturbed mind, aloud or silently to ourselves. We repeat this process eight more times for the rest of the day. Altogether, we should do one round of ten recitations, nine times a day, every day as follows:

1. Upon waking up
2. Before starting breakfast

3. After finishing breakfast
4. Before work
5. Before starting lunch
6. After finishing lunch
7. Before starting dinner
8. After finishing dinner
9. At bedtime

Altogether, this method is practiced nine times daily. The key is regularity; disruption of this practice will reduce its effectiveness. Without interruption, the cultivator will soon feel an increase in his/her purity of mind and wisdom.

Diligent practice of the Ten-Recitation Method, together with unwavering belief and vows, can ensure fulfillment of our wish to reach the Western Pure Land of Infinite Life and Infinite Light. We hope everyone will practice accordingly.

Namo Amitabha!

Glossary

Aeon. 1,334,000,000 years. Often expressed as the time it would take for a mountain of solid rock of ten cubic leagues to wear down if the tip of a heavenly maiden's delicate tunic brushed against it every hundred years. A fantastically long period of time.

Affliction. Condition or cause of pain, distress and suffering which disturbs the body and mind.

Amitabha (Sanskrit or Skrt). The name of the Buddha of the Western Pure Land, primarily meaning Infinite Life and Light.

Anuttara-Samyak-Sambodhi (Skrt). Highest, proper and complete enlightenment.

Arhat (Skrt). One who has reached self-realization, a state in which one possesses no erroneous perceptions, views, speech or behavior.

Attachments. Fixed to certain ideas or

objects.

Bodhi mind (Skrt). The great compassionate and sincere mind, with every thought to attain complete self-realization for self and other.

Bodhisattva (Skrt). One who helps others to reach realization after achieving their own.

Buddha (Skrt). One who has reached perfection in both self-realization and helping others to reach realization.

Delusion. False beliefs, wrong views.

Dharma (Skrt). 1) The teachings of the Buddha (generally capitalized in English); 2) Things, events, phenomena, everything; 3) Duty, law, doctrine.

Dharma-ending Age. The Dharma Perfect Age began with Buddha Shakyamuni's demise and lasted five hundred years, during which Enlightenment was often attained. The Dharma Semblance Age began after that and lasted one thousand years, during which Enlightenment was seldom attained. The Dharma Ending Age that we are now in began after that and will last for ten thousand years during which Enlightenment will rarely be attained.

Dusts. Metaphor for all the mundane things that can cloud our self-nature.

Eight Afflictions. Absence of embarrassment and shamefulness, and the presence of jealously, stinginess, misdeeds, drowsiness, sleep and agitation.

Eighth Ground Bodhisattva. There are ten levels or grounds of a Bodhisattva's enlightenment which summarize the most important steps in a Bodhisattva's path right before attaining buddhahood. Some say it is at this level that Bodhisattvas reach the stage of Non-regression, the level at which they will never retreat from the Bodhisattva-path.

Four Universal Vows of Buddhas and Bodhisattvas. (1) Sentient beings are innumerable, I vow to help them all; (2)

Afflictions are inexhaustible, I vow to end them all: (3) Ways to practice are boundless, I vow to master them all: (4) Enlightenment is unsurpassable, I vow to attain it.

Five Desires. Wealth, lust, food-drink, fame and sleep.

Five Guidelines. Following: 1) The Three Conditions; 2) The Six Principles of Harmony; 3) The Three Learnings; 4) The Six Paramitas or Principles and 5) Samantabhadra Bodhisattva's Ten Great Vows.

Five Pure Land Sutras and One Sastra. (1) <u>The Buddha Speaks of the Infinite Life Sutra of Adornment, Purity, Equality and Enlightenment of the Mahayana School,</u> (2) <u>The Amitabha Sutra,</u> (3) <u>The Visualization Sutra,</u> (4) The Chapter of Universal Worthy Bodhisattva's Conduct and Vows, (5) The Chapter on the Perfect Complete Realization of Great Strength Bodhisattva through Buddha Name Recitation from the

Surangama Sutra and (6) Vasubandhu Bodhisattva's Report on the Way to Reaching the Pure Land.

<u>Good Fortune</u>. Happiness, intelligence, wellbeing, prosperity etc.

<u>Good roots</u>. Good qualities or seeds sown by a good life to be reaped later.

<u>Hungry Ghost</u>. One of the three lower realms. Hungry ghosts wander in a limbo-like state in which they can find no satisfaction for their desires, especially but not exclusively, for their hunger or thirst. One is reborn here if he or she has extreme greed.

<u>Karma</u> (Skrt). Law of Cause and Effect, results from thought, speech and behavior.

<u>Karmic Result</u>. The natural reward or retribution brought about by the Law of Cause and Effect (Karma).

<u>Mahayana</u> (Skrt). One of the two major branches of Buddhism. Bodhisattva path of helping all sentient beings to attain universal liberation.

Merits. The great benefits (wealth, intelligence, etc) of the human and celestial realms; therefore, they are temporary and subject to birth and death. **Virtues**, on the other hand, are attained from one's pure mind and enable one to transcend birth and death and lead to Buddhahood. An identical action, e.g. charity, can lead either to merit or virtue, depending on the mind of the practitioner, whether he or she is seeking ordinary rewards (merit) or transcendence (virtue).

Mindfulness of Buddha. Initially the mind remembers the Buddha and does not forget. After further cultivation, one constantly contemplates the Buddha.

Nine Realms. All ten realms minus the Buddha realm.

Non-regression. One who will never retreat from the Bodhisattva-path, some say it is not reached until the eighth of the ten grounds of a Bodhisattva.

Phenomena. Things, events, happenings, everything.

Prajna-Wisdom (Skrt). Intuitive wisdom.

Pratyekabuddha (Skrt). One who attains his enlightenment alone, independent of a teacher, with the objective of attaining Nirvana for him/herself.

Precepts. Rules set up by Buddha Shakyamuni to guide his students from erroneous thoughts, speech and behavior.

Pure Land. See Western Pure Land.

Pure Mind or Purity of Mind. The mind without discrimination or attachments.

Retribution. Karmic punishment from erroneous thought, speech or action.

Saha world (Skrt). Refers to our solar system, filled with suffering and afflictions, yet gladly endured by its inhabitants.

Samadhi (Skrt). Meditative absorption. Usually denotes the particular final stage of pure concentration and contemplation. There are many degrees and types of Samadhi.

Sangha (Skrt). Group of four or more peoples who properly practice the Buddha's teaching together, especially The Six Principles of Harmony.

Sanskrit (Skrt). Language of ancient India.

Sastra (Skrt). Commentary on sutras primarily by Bodhisattvas.

Self-Nature. Our original, true self that we still have, but is currently covered by deluded thoughts.

Sentient being. A living being that is aware of itself and can experience feeling or sensation.

Sharira (Skrt). Relics that remain after cremation indicating the person had attained some degree of purity of body and mind.

Six Paramitas or Principles. Giving, precept observation, patience, diligence, concentration and wisdom.

Six Principles of Harmony. 1) Share the

same viewpoints or goals. 2) Observe the same precepts. 3) Live and practice together harmoniously. 4) Not quarrel. 5) Experience the inner peace and happiness from practicing together harmoniously. 6) To share benefits equally.

Six Realms. Three upper realms are heavens, asuras and humans. Three lower realms are animals, hungry ghosts and hells.

Six Senses. Sight, sound, smell, taste, touch and mind object.

Six Sense Objects. Form, sound, scent, taste, texture and mind object.

Six Sense Organs. Eyes, ears, nose, mouth, body and mind.

Sutra (Skrt). Teaching by the Buddha, initially given verbally, later compiled and written down by the Buddha's students.

Ten Directions. North, Northeast, East, Southeast, South, Southwest, West, Northwest, above and below.

Ten Good Conducts. No killing, stealing, sexual misconduct, lying, abusive language, backbiting, seductive words, greed, anger or ignorance.

Ten Great Vows of Samantabhadra Bodhisattva. 1) Pay respect to all Buddhas. 2) Praise "Thus Come One." 3) Make offerings extensively. 4) Repent of Karmic obstacles. 5) Be joyful over others meritorious deeds. 6) Appeal to the Buddha to turn the Dharma wheel. 7) Request the Buddha to reside in this world. 8) Constantly be a diligent follower of the Buddha's teaching. 9) Accord with all sentient beings. 10) Dedicate all merits.

Ten Realms. Six realms plus those of Buddhas, Bodhisattvas, Pratyeka-buddhas and Sound-hearers.

Three Conditions. The first includes being filial and respectful to one's parents and teachers, being compassionate and not killing any living beings and the Ten Good Conducts. The second is following the Three Refuges, precepts, laws and customs, and conducting oneself in a proper and dignified manner. Third is generating the Bodhi mind, deeply believing in the Law of Cause and Effect, reciting and upholding Mahayana sutras, and encouraging others to advance on the path to Enlightenment.

Three Learnings. Self-discipline, concentration and wisdom.

Three Poisons. Greed, anger and ignorance.

Three Refuges. We take refuge in the Buddha, Dharma and Sangha. When we take refuge in the Buddha, we are returning from our deluded state of mind and relying upon an awakened, understanding mind. When we take refuge in the Dharma, we are returning from deviant views and relying upon proper views and understanding. When we take refuge in the Sangha, we are returning from pollution and disharmony and relying upon purity of mind and the Six Principles of Harmony.

Transliteration. To represent (letters or words) in the corresponding characters of another alphabet, so the original sound is retained.

Virtues. See Merits.

Way Place. Usually called a temple, a place where Buddhist practitioners come to practice.

Western Pure Land. World created by Buddha Amitabha. An ideal place of cultivation, those who are born there are no longer subject to reincarnation.

The Teachings of Great Master Yin Guang

Whether a lay or a left home person, one needs to respect elders and be harmonious with those around him/her. One endures what others cannot and practices what others cannot achieve. One should labor on behalf of others and help them to succeed in their undertakings. While sitting quietly, one reflects upon one's own faults. When chatting with friends do not discuss the rights and wrongs of others. In every action one makes, whether dressing or eating, from dawn to dusk and dusk to dawn, one recites the Buddha's name. Aside from Buddha name recitation, whether reciting quietly or silently, one does not give rise to improper thoughts. If wandering thoughts arise, one immediately dismisses them. Constantly maintain a humble and repentant heart; even if one has upheld true cultivation, one still feels their practice is shallow and never boasts. One should mind one's own business and not the business of others. Only see the good examples of others instead of their shortcomings. One would do well to see oneself as ordinary and everyone else as Bodhisattvas. If one can cultivate according to these teachings, one is sure to reach the Western Pure Land of Ultimate Bliss.

Homage to Amitabha! Amitabha!

"Wherever the Buddha's teachings have flourished, either in cities or countrysides, people would gain inconceivable benefits. The land and people would be enveloped in peace. The sun and moon will shine clear and bright. Wind and rain would appear accordingly, and there will be no disasters. Nations would be prosperous and there would be no use for soldiers or weapons. People would abide by morality and accord with laws. They would be courteous and humble. Everyone would be content and there would be no injustice. There would be no thefts or violence. The strong would not dominate the weak and everyone would get their fair share."

❧ THE BUDDHA SPEAKS OF THE INFINITE LIFE SUTRA OF ADORNMENT, PURITY, EQUALITY AND ENLIGHTENMENT OF THE MAHAYANA SCHOOL ❧

With bad advisors forever left behind,
From paths of evil he departs for eternity,
Soon to see the Buddha of Limitless Light
And perfect Samantabhadra's Supreme Vows.

The supreme and endless blessings
of Samantabhadra's deeds,
I now universally transfer.
May every living being, drowning and adrift,
Soon return to the Land of
Limitless Light!

The Vows of Samantabhadra

I vow that when my life approaches its end,
All obstructions will be swept away;
I will see Amitabha Buddha,
And be born in his Land of Ultimate Bliss and Peace.

When reborn in the Western Land,
I will perfect and completely fulfill
Without exception these Great Vows,
To delight and benefit all beings.

The Vows of Samantabhadra
Avatamsaka Sutra

Collected Talks of Ven. Master Chin Kung

淨空法師專集

淨空法師專集有聲版網址：http://www.amtb.org.tw

達拉斯佛教會網址：http:// www.amtb-dba.org

美國淨宗學會網址：http://www.amtb-usa.org

新加坡淨宗學會即時講演網址：http://www.amtb.org.sg

新加坡佛教居士林即時講演網址：http://www.amtb1.org.sg

【閱讀專集內容之方法】

◈ 連接 Internet，打開網路瀏覽程式，例如：IE

◈ 在 Open Location Line 下，輸入網路位址：
www.amtb.org.tw

【收聽講演之方法】

◈ 至專集〝有聲版〞內，選擇講演之題目即可收聽。

◈ 可參考網站中有聲版內所附之說明。

阿彌陀佛 • 阿彌陀佛 • 阿彌陀佛 • 阿彌陀佛 • 阿彌陀佛 。

達拉斯佛教會

Dallas Buddhist Association, Inc.

515 Apollo Road, Richardson, TX 75081 U.S.A.

Tel: (972) 234-4401   Fax: (972) 234-8342

新加坡淨宗學會

Amitabha Buddhist Society (Singapore)

No. 2, Lorong 35 Geylang, Singapore 387934

Tel: (65) 744-7444   Fax: (65) 744-4774

新加坡佛教居士林

The Singapore Buddhist Lodge

17-19 Kim Yam Road Singapore 239329

Tel: (65) 737-2630   Fax: (65) 737-0877

List of Buddhist Organizations

For enquires or orders, please contact your nearest centre.

AUSTRALIA

THE AMITABHA BUDDHIST ASSOCIATION OF QUEENSLAND INC. (AUSTRALIA)
11 TOONA PLACE CALAMVALE, BRISBANE,
QLD 4116 AUSTRALIA
Tel: 61-7-32731693; Fax: 61-7-32720677

**BUDDHIST COUNCIL
OF NEW SOUTH WALES INC.**
P.O. BOX 224 BURWOOD NSW 2134 AUSTRALIA
SHOP 82, BKK CENTRE, EVANS AVENUE,
EASTLAKES, NSW, 2018, AUSTRALIA
Tel.:61-2-96933053; Fax: 61-2-96931146

BANGLADESH

ATTADEEPA FOUNDATION, BANGLADESH
ANANDA VIHARA, TABALCHARI, RANGAMATI,
RANGAMANTI MUNICIPALITY,
RANGAMATI HILL TRACTS,
POST CODE NO. 4500, BOX NO. 21, BANGLADESH
Tel: 880-351-2395; Fax: 880-351-2395, 880-610420

**MAHAMANDAL WELFARE ORGANIZATION
(MWO), BANGLADESH**
G.P.O. BOX No. 1100 P.S. CHITTAGONG
HATHAZARI DIST. CHITTAGONG, BANGLADESH
Tel: 880-31-208229, 208405; Fax: 880-31-225200

CANADA

**VANCOUVER YUAN YUNG BUDDHISM
CENTRE SOCIETY**
3642 KINGSWAY, VANCOUVER B.C.
CANADA V5R 5M2
Tel: 604-434-1223; Fax:604-4341223

**THE CHAM SHAN
BUDDHIST LIBRARY AND GALARY**
1224 LAWRENCE AVENUE WEST NORTH YORK,
ONTARIO M6A 1E4, CANADA
Tel:416-7841357, 2259228; Fax: 416-7899025

ENGLAND

AMARAVATI BUDDHIST MONASTERY
GREAT GADDESDEN, HEMEL HEMPSTEAD
HERTFORDSHIRE HP1 3BZ ENGLAND
Tel;44-2842455; Fax:44-2843721

BUDDHIST EDUCATION FOUNDATION U.K.
18 HUSON CLOSE, HAMPSTEAD,
LONDON NW3 3JW, ENGLAND
Tel:171-5866923, 1268-540522; FaX: 171-7948594

THE LONDON BUDDHIST VIHARA
DHARMAPALA BUILDING, THE AVENUE,
BEDFORD PARK CHISWICK
LONDON W4 1UD, ENGLAND
Tel:44-181-9959493; FaX:44-181-9948130

FRANCE

INTERNATIONAL BUDDHIST ASSOCIATION
7, CITE FIRMIN BOURGEOIS,
LE BOURGET 93350, FRANCE
Tel:33-1-48- 351071, 352249; Fax:33-1-48-376314

**PAGODE LINH SON
(LINH SON TEMPLE/PARIS)**
9 AVE JEAN JAURES 94340 JOINVILLE LE PONT,
FRANCE
Tel:33-1-48-837547; Fax:1-48837759

HONG KONG

BUDDHIST YOUTH ASSOCIATION LTD.
144 BOUNDARY STREET, 2/F., KOWLOON,
HONG KONG
Tel: 852-23360437; Fax:23361851, 4806120

INDIA

MAHA BODHI SOCIETY
14, KALIDASA ROAD, GANDHINAGAR,
BANGALORE-560 009, INDIA
Tel: 91-812-260684, 250684; Fax:91-80-2264438, 2250292

**BAUDDHA PRASHIKSHAN SANSTHAN,
BUDDHA BHOOMI**
KAMPTEE-NAGPUR G.N. ROAD P.O. KHAIRI-
441002, DIST. NAGPUR, (M.S.) INDIA
Tel: 91-7109-88732, 91-712-640360; Fax:91-7109-88707

VIPASSANA RESEARCH INSTITUTE
DHAMMAGIRI, IGATPURI -422 403, DIST. NASHIKA,
MAHARASHTRA, INDIA.
Tel:91-2553-84076, 84086, 84302; Fax:91-2553-84176

WORLD BUDDHIST MISSION
S. NO. 124 , JADHAV WASTI, KALAS,
PUNE 411 015, INDIA
Tel:91-212-887447; Fax:91-212-313268

DHAMMACHAKRA PRAVARTAN MAHAVIHAR
MAHAVIHAR, RAJA HARISHCHANDRA RD,
DAPODI, PUNE-411 012, INDIA
Tel:91-212-318174,312919; Fax: 91-212-313268

ANANDA BUDDHA VIHARA TRUST
SAINAGAR, TUKARAM GATE, NORTH
LALLAGUDA, SECUNDERABAD-500 017 A.P. INDIA
Tel:91-40-7732421; Fax: 91-40-842477

MAHA BODHI SOCIETY
17, KENNET LANE, EGMORE,
MADRAS-600 008, INDIA
Tel:44-8252458

INTERNATIONAL BROTHERHOOD MISSION
MAHABODHI VIHAR JYOTINAGAR (NALIAPOOL),
DIBRUGARH-786001 ASSAM, INDIA
Tel: 91-373-23014, 20145; Fax:91-373-22300

MACAU

MACAU BUDDHIST YOUTH CENTRE
AV, HORTA E COSTA 90B 1 F EDF,
POU ON-MACAU
Tel:853-211733, 533894; Fax:853-750096, 573672

MALAYSIA

PERSATUAN PENGANUT AGAMA BUDDA AMITABHA (MALAYSIA)
16-A, FIRST FLOOR, JLN PAHANG 53000 KUALA LUMPUR, MALAYSIA
Tel:60-3-4414101; Fax:60-3-4412172

BUDDHIST MISSIONARY SOCIETY
123 JALAN BERHALA, OFF JALAN TUN SAMBANTHAN, 50470 KUALA LUMPUR, MALAYSIA.
Tel: 60-3-2741886, 60-3-2741889; Fax:60-3-2733835

WISDOM AUDIO VISUAL EXCHANGE, W.A.V.E.
No 2, JALAN CHAN AH THONG OFF JLN TUN SAMBANTHAN 50470 KUALA LUMPUR, MALAYSIA
Tel: 60-3-2749509

MYANMAR

CHINESE BUDDHIST TEMPLE
SHWEGONDINE ROAD, BAHAN T/S. YANGON, MYANMAR
Tel:95-1-549608

DHAMMA JOTI VIPASSANA CENTRE, INTERNATIONAL DHAMMAGIRI VIPASSANA ASSOCIATION
WINGABA YELE KYAUNG, NGAHTATGYI PAGODA (CAMBLE) ROAD, BAHAN TOWNSHIP, YANGON, MYANMAR
Tel: 95-1549290; Fax:95-1-289965, 95-1-524983

NEPAL

NAGARJUNA INSTITUTE OF EXACT METHODS
(A CENTRE FOR BUDDHIST STUDIES)
P.O. BOX 100 CHAKUPAT, LALITPUR KATHMANDU, NEPAL
Tel:997-1-520558; Fax:997-1-527446

SRIKIRTI VIHARA (SIRIKITTI VIHAR)
KIRTIPUR, KATHMANDU, NEPAL
Tel: 977-1-330836; Fax: 977-1-330889

BIR-PURNA PUSTAK SANGRAHALAY
GABAHAL, LALITPUR-18, NEPAL
Tel: 977-1-533326, 533077; Fax: 977-1-527446, 533326

NEW ZEALAND

BODHIN YANARAMA BUDDHIST MONASTERY
17 RAKAU GROVE, STOKES VALLEY, WEILLINGTON, 6008 NEW ZEALAND
Tel:64-4-5637193; Fax: 64-4-5635125

TSI MING BUDDHIST TEMPLE
17 WAIRAKEI STREET GREENLANE AUCKLAND, NEW ZEALAND
Tel: 64-9-5798758; Fax:64-9-5799138

NORWAY

VIETNAMESE BUDDHIST ORGANIZATION IN NORWAY, KHUONG VIET TEMPLE
BLYSTADVN 2, 2006 LOVENSTAD, NORWAY
Tel:47-67-973033; Fax:47-67-971905

PHILIPPINES

UNIVERSAL WISDOM FOUNDATION RESOURCE CENTER

12-B DONA JUANA RODRIGUEZ AVE., (BROADWAY) NEW MANILA, QUEZON CITY, PHILIPPINES
Tel: 632-7224750, 7226425; Fax:632-7254908, 72155

POLAND

THE BUDDHIST MISSION IN POLAND
ul. Slaska 12/12 , 70-432 Szczecin, POLAND
Tel:48-91-4880289; Fax: 48-91-880289, 48-91-488028

SINGAPORE

AMITABHA BUDDHIST SOCIETY (SINGAPOR
NO. 2 LORONG 35 GEYLANG SINGAPORE 3879.
Tel:65-744-7444; Fax: 65-744-4774

SINGAPORE BUDDHIST MEDITATION CENTRE
No.1, JALAN MAS PUTEH SINGAPORE-128607
Tel:65-7783330; Fax:65-7730150

SOUTH AFRICA

NAN HUA TEMPLE
P.O. BOX 741 BRONKHORSTSPRUIT 1020 R.S.A.;
Tel:27-13-9310009; Fax: 27-13-9310013

SPAIN

AMITABHA BUDDHIST SOCIETY (SPAIN)
C/ VALVERDE 5, 28004 MADRID, SPAIN
Tel:341-5222603,34-91-5223603; Fax:34-91-5227151

SRI LANKA

DHARMA CHAKKRA CHILD FOUNDATION
GONAPOLA ROAD VEEDAGAMA BANDARAGAMA SRI LANKA
Tel:94-3-491771 ; 94-1-853733; Fax:94-1-508616

THAILAND

BHOMAN-KHUNARAM TEMPLE
323 SOI 19 WAT BHOMAN SATHU PRADIT ROAD, YANNAWA BANKOK 10120 THAILAND
Tel:2117885, 2112363; Fax:662-2127777

USA

AMITABHA BUDDHIST SOCIETY OF USA
650 S. BERNARDO AVE. SUNNYVALE, CA 94087, USA
Tel:408-7363386; Fax:408-7363389

AMIDA SOCIETY
5918 CLOVERLY AVE., TEMPLE CITY CA, 91780 US
Tel:626-2865700; Fax:626-2867988

AMITABHA BUDDHIST SOCIETY OF PHILADELPHIA (IN ORGANIZATION)
1010 ARCH 3FL., PHILA. PA. 19107 USA
Tel:O:215-9232388, 215-9231006; Fax:215-9235106

THE BUDDHIST ASSOCIATION OF THE UNITED STATES
Rd #13, ROUTE 301 CARMEL, NY 10512 USA
Tel: 914-2251819, 2256117; Fax:914-2250447 , 914-2251819

DALLAS BUDDHIST ASSOCIATION,INC
515 APOLLO ROAD, RICHARDSON, TX 75081 U
Tel:972-2344401; Fax:972-2348342

DEDICATION OF MERIT

May the merit and virtue
accrued from this work
adorn the Buddha's Pure Land,
repay the four great kindnesses above,
and relieve the suffering of
those on the three paths below.

May those who see or hear of these efforts
generate Bodhi-mind,
spend their lives devoted to the Buddha Dharma,
and finally be reborn together in
the Land of Ultimate Bliss.
Homage to Amita Buddha!

NAMO AMITABHA

南無阿彌陀佛

Reprinted and Donated for free distribution by
The Corporate Body of the Buddha Educational Foundation
11 F., 55 Hang Chow South Road Sec 1, Taipei, Taiwan, R.O.C.
Tel: 886-2-23951198 , Fax: 886-2-23913415
Email: overseas@budaedu.org.tw
Printed in Taiwan
1999 September, 37500 copies

EN107-1632